Territorio, storia e passione.
Ecco tre elementi indispensabili
per ottenere dalle olive un
grande extravergine.
Il territorio è quello siciliano,
che offre una ricchezza unica
di emozioni; la storia è quella
che vuole l'ulivo radicato
nell'Isola da oltre tremila anni;
la passione è quella di una
famiglia, i Barbera, che
da più di un secolo attraverso
quattro generazioni si tramanda
l'amore per la terra ed i suoi
preziosi frutti.
È naturale poi che questa
filosofia abbia sposato
la cucina di un grande chef
come Nino Graziano, il patron
del Mulinazzo, che ha fatto
dei prodotti del "suo"
territorio un punto di forza.
Una sinergia nel nome
del buon gusto.
Felici di essere al suo fianco,
orgogliosi di arricchire le sue
creazioni. Semplicemente
con il nostro olio extravergine.

www.oliobarbera.com

Manfredi Barbera

Editing: Studio Pro.Bel
Photography: Janez Pukšič
Graphic design: Dante Albieri
Translation: Liz Marcucci Zazzera

© Bibliotheca Culinaria S.r.l.
Viale Genova 2/B
26900 Lodi Italy
Tel. 0371-412684
Fax 0371-413287
info@bibliothecaculinaria.it

ISBN 88-86174-54-3

1° edition - November 2003

MY SICILIAN COOKING

Nino Graziano

Preface
Jean-Georges Klein
Introduction
Fabrizio Carrera
Photography
Janez Pukšič

BIBLIOTHECA CULINARIA

Italy: how much happiness is enclosed in this single word!
The sun, the sea, the hospitality, the culture, the food: the
choice is difficult once you have crossed the Alps.
But really, how can anyone resist the food? A new generation of
Italian chefs has made a virtue of travel and has learned a great
deal without betraying the past. Italian cuisine is still very much
modeled on home-style cooking and the influence of
generations of grandmothers, but these young chefs have set
themselves the additional goal of giving this sound base a
creative twist.
The innate aesthetic sensibility of the Italians has transformed
even the trattoria into a sophisticated dining space.
Nino Graziano is very much a part of this new generation and
he has never hesitated to put his cooking on the line, to dare
where others are content to perpetuate the status quo. His
motto: Move people, touch them with your cooking. He
succeeds in doing this by applying his imagination to traditional
Sicilian cuisine. This very subtle balance between tradition and
innovation most clearly characterizes the cooking of my friend
Nino and on that front, we understand one another perfectly.

Jean-Georges Klein
L'Arnsbourg
Baerenthal, September 2003

His identity card defines him quite simply as "chef", but there is more to Nino Graziano than this label implies. The chef patron of Il Mulinazzo plies his trade in Villafrati, a tiny town off the highway that connects Palermo to Agrigento. No matter what dish he happens to be preparing, no matter how much frenetic activity whirls about his now famous kitchen, Nino remains focussed on offering an emotional experience. He is intent upon concentrating visual, olfactory and gustatory sensations into something more than a sum of stimuli.

A creator of emotions might, in fact, be a better definition for this chef who, in just a few years, has managed to become a major player in the Italian restaurant scene. Certainly he is the chef who has aroused the most interest among colleagues and enlightened diners alike. This is true perhaps because he so completely incarnates the Sicilian stereotype with his black mustache, his gesturing, his slow, measured way of speaking, his curious penetrating black eyes and his notable humility (not a bad trait in a trade noted for its egos). It is also true because his cuisine offers a resounding confirmation of the importance of the territorial bond that continues to sustain the finest Italian cooking. Sicily represents the great unexplored territory yet to be discovered.

Certainly, there is talent in Nino's cooking, but there is also a great deal of research into the island's many fine ingredients. The list of dishes that he has rediscovered or reinvented in a modern key is a long one, but his signature dish should suffice as an example: *Macco di fave con scampi e ricotta* (*Purée of fava beans with scampi and ricotta*). *Macco* is the Sicilian version of the Italian *passato*, which refers to a preparation that has been passed through a sieve. In this case the finest cooked legumes (fresh or dried) are reduced to a purée and enriched with scampi and a drizzle of (rigorously Sicilian) extra virgin olive oil. This is not merely delicious; it is the essence of the island in a single dish, an emotional experience for even the most jaded gourmet.

Nino Graziano is not a one-dimensional character defined by his trade. Each of us carries in his or her professional baggage something of our family legacy, our personal interests and our singular sensibility. Travel and soccer have played important roles in Nino's professional career, but it is necessary to return to the beginning of his story to see just how this occurred. Nino was born in Bolognetta, another small town in the Palermo hinterland, not far from Villafrati. His father worked the land; his mother was the center of their home. With his two brothers and a sister they formed a typical Sicilian family, their lives revolving around the land, their small economies and their familial affections. When he finished junior high Nino decided to continue his studies, a step that meant commuting to Palermo every day. His father encouraged him to enroll in hotel school, not only because it was considered a fairly sure route to finding a job, but also so that he would not "die of hunger." Nino recalls, "I went off to school and in a couple of years I achieved the status of apprentice chef. My first job landed me in the kitchen of a restaurant in Mondello for the summer season." This fashionable beach resort of the Palermitani, with its villas from the Liberty period was also the preferred destination for waves of weekend bathers from the city's working class, Nino recalls, "I began cleaning squid at ten in the morning and finished at ten at night. It seemed as though I did nothing else." A passion for travel and a youthful desire to seek new experiences, inspired the not yet eighteen year old Nino to seek employment abroad. "I received an offer to work in an Italian trattoria in Lausanne and didn't have to think twice. In any case, my decision to become a chef was in part motivated by the idea that the job would allow me to travel a great deal. I was fortunate that one of my first positions was in Switzerland. There I discovered a

completely different world. Lausanne seemed light years away from all that I had known.

A wealthy city, it seemed populated by beautiful people and it presented many opportunities to enjoy oneself. It was my ticket to learning to speak French and even though there was work to be done, there was also free time for friends and the disco. There for the first time I worked as part of a team of chefs. There were seven of us and I discovered there was a great deal of respect for the role. With a day and a half off every week, to me it felt like quite a conquest."

But Nino did not stop there. Each winter he went home to Sicily. He did his obligatory military service and worked for a brief period in the resort city of Rimini. There he met some French colleagues and they hit it off instantly. A job offer from the other side of the Alps was quick to arrive and Nino was seriously considering it. He went back to Sicily to think it over and found himself with yet another offer: a starting position with Misilmeri, a minor league soccer team. The salary of two and a half million lira per month was nothing to scoff at in 1975 and the team's owner even offered to eventually find him a full time job as a chef if he had second thoughts. Nino was obviously tempted.

The team position seemed to enclose all of the known quantities: a stable job, proximity to family, Sicily – but the following day he was on his way to France, specifically to Metz, an important city in the Alsace-Lorraine region. His adventures had begun.

Nino went to work in a large hotel that included a restaurant and a disco. "The cuisine was international and I did my part with dignity."

At this point, Nino recalls, "I was twenty three and looking to have a good time." After work there was dancing and a lot of youthful hijinks. His two closest friends proposed a joint venture – opening an Italian restaurant. Together they found a rustic building near a forest. With help from the city, they remodeled it and so began a real adventure: *Papiermühle*. The Paper Mill's specialties were spaghetti and lasagna. "It was a great learning experience," quips the chef of Il Mulinazzo.

The term "Italian chef" means absolutely nothing in France. Right or wrong the French believe themselves to be the world's finest practitioners of the culinary arts. Even today they look down on the Italian restaurant scene. Despite this, it went well. Those were extraordinary years. The restaurant was a big success.

We had a capacity for one hundred twenty and we were full from morning to night." And soccer? "I didn't exactly hang up my playing shoes. I played for Metz in the C league. The game was with me after all and it turned out to be a great way to expand our clientele."

In France Nino met his future wife Sabine Bour and it was she who represented a real turning point. The daughter of restaurateurs, she became more than a faithful helpmate in Nino's professional life. His most important advisor, she played a major role in the decision making that followed. Today she is the guiding force of the dining room at Il Mulinazzo. Her firmness and efficiency pervade the restaurant. Still based in France, they married in 1980. Not long after, Nino succumbed to one of those nostalgic crises that can only happen to Sicilians (islanders in their souls). "At a certain point," he explains, "I started to miss the light, the sun, the heat.

I was homesick for Sicily." The couple headed south, but not straight for Sicily. In Ventimiglia they stopped to visit Nino's aunt and ended up staying. There they felt as though they had found the best of both worlds, France and Italy. The Mediterranean was once more in site and the climate was gentler. For a honeymoon there would be time later; Nino had already found work. In Menton, he bought a pizzeria for twenty-seven million lira and they were off and running again. Their initial venture as a couple, the restaurant offered international cuisine in addition to the ever-present pizza. Here too things went well. Nino played on the local soccer team in Bordighera and the restaurant was soon overflowing with teammates and friends. Yet, in three years they were ready to raise the stakes. They sold the combination restaurant-pizzeria and acquired a larger restaurant in Ventimiglia. For the first time Nino was not enjoying his work which seemed repetitious and monotonous. When their old friends from Metz encouraged them to return, the couple headed back to Alsace-Lorraine. But, nothing was the same. *Papiermühle* was only a fond memory.

When he met Georges Smith, the chef of a restaurant not far from Metz, Nino was poised for a change. This important relationship drew him into the world of haute cuisine and marked a period of significant growth. The team forward, the kid from Bolognetta, the aspiring chef who wanted to see the world grew up.

The accumulated layers of professional experience, relationships and travel had sedimented. Over time, a

personal concept of haute cuisine gradually took shape, as did the realization that there were really no secrets. It was passion that fueled the most successful chefs.

At the end of the 1980s the Graziano family (now with two children, Elena and Deborah, in tow) moved yet again. This time they really did head South, to Sicily. It was time to go home. Nino was ready to start over again. We should recall that the Sicily he returned to had yet to establish itself on the gastronomic scene. Its wine boom was still very much in the future. Nino and Sabine opened their restaurant on the important artery that joined Palermo to Agrigento. Little by little, the modest square building improved its appearance and became more welcoming. Situated among the high hills that surround Palermo, it offered a view of sunburned fields, scattered hill towns and the stately passage of life tied to the agricultural calendar. Here Nino concentrated on creating a Sicilian cuisine that would cast an ironic glance at its French counterpart. Hardly an easy task, it demanded a great deal of reinvention, study, comparison and tasting. Sabine proved to be an essential assistant as she had both a discriminating eye and palate. There was, of course, the problem of provisions. The fish? Freshness is not always a given, even on an island in a town just a few kilometers from the ocean. Nino remained undaunted. He redoubled his efforts until he had established a relationship with the market at Porticello, a coastal town with the largest fishing fleet in the province. And the ricotta? The process was repeated until he had found the finest cheesemaker in the district. These are but two examples, but they are emblematic.

Dishes were short-lived on the menu. Nino was in constant motion, creating and re-creating from morning to night. Slowly, he built a clientele, but is also quick to confess, "At the outset, things were very difficult. It was hard for us to undermine some very basic concepts about Sicilian cooking, to make people understand that the long cooking and heavy-handed seasoning they were accustomed to needed to be abandoned. When I said these things, they looked at me with suspicion." But, recognition did eventually arrive. The gastronomic guides began to take note of the unassuming restaurant off the highway, citing its interesting cuisine. From the close of the 1990s the consensus has mounted to in an ever-rising crescendo as the various elements of the specialized press "discovered" the Mulinazzo phenomenon. It was a propitious moment because it coincided with the media's discovery of the wine of Sicily. The wine-food connection was inevitable and Nino was soon acclaimed as one of the principal forces behind the island's gastronomic Renaissance. The Espresso Restaurant Guide ranked Il Mulinazzo as the top Sicilian restaurant. Word began to spread beyond the island. Even today Nino recalls with a note of pride the Japanese diner who took the 30-kilometer taxi ride from Palermo's top hotel to dine at his restaurant (leaving the driver waiting for the return trip). It was an expensive undertaking, but the Japanese man was willing to make the investment to dine at Il Mulinazzo. From that time it was not long until he was granted his second Michelin star, a fitting accolade for a lifetime of sacrifice, a fine accomplishment not only for the chef who has best interpreted the island's flavors, but for Sicily as well.

Nino and Sabine's achievement came at a very important juncture for Sicily, a fortunate moment. "After the dark years in which the island was associated only with the Mafia, people have begun to associate it with something positive. Rather than ask who was killed where, tourists are now more likely to inquire about a particular grape variety, the late ripening peaches or a rare cheese. We have extraordinary ingredients at our disposal transformed by artisans and not by agribusiness. This guarantees real flavor." For this reason as well, Sicily is being talked about in a new way.

That's all there is to it. No alchemy, no tricks, no special effects. This is a simple story about a chef, a creator of emotions, an enthusiast for his work, insatiably curious. "My secret? There are no secrets in this line of work," Nino replies. "The other day I read an interview with Claudio Abbado, the famous conductor. When asked what it means to be young, he replied, "To have passion. To trust one's instincts and hurl oneself into the breach." In my small way I try to do the same and perhaps that is what makes me feel young. Passion is the driving force and perhaps there is something to be said for the concept of striving to make others happy. If my cooking makes people happy, then so am I."

Fabrizio Carrera

Purée of fava beans with scampi and ricotta

Serves 4

8 scampi
all-purpose flour
extra virgin olive oil

Fava bean purée
300 g (10 1/2 oz) peeled dried fava beans*
1 lt (1 quart) water
150 g (5 1/3 oz) Swiss chard
1/2 onion
1 celery rib
1 clove of garlic
1 tomato
50 g (1 3/4 oz) wild fennel**
1 tablespoon extra virgin olive oil
100 g (3 1/2 oz) sheep's milk ricotta
dash of hot red pepper
salt

Garnish
70 g (2 1/2 oz) speck***
croutons
a few sprigs of wild fennel
1 tablespoon extra virgin olive oil
freshly ground pepper

Soak the fava beans in cold water for 24 hours, drain them and transfer them to a stockpot containing 1 lt (1 quart) of simmering water. Allow them to boil for 5 minutes, skimming any impurities that rise to the surface. Add the roughly chopped Swiss chard, onion, celery, garlic, tomato, wild fennel and olive oil and simmer for 2 hours. Transfer the fava beans, the vegetables, and their cooking liquid to a food processor and blend in batches with the ricotta and hot red pepper to obtain a dense yet finely-grained purée. Salt to taste.

In the meantime, shell the scampi and toss them in the flour until they are just coated. Briefly sauté them in a little extra virgin olive oil and reserve warm.
Julienne the speck and heat it in a non-stick pan to melt the fat. Drain on paper towels and reserve warm.

Presentation Place a ladle of the fava bean mixture in the center of each plate. Top with 2 scampi, a sprinkling of croutons, a few strips of crisp speck and a little wild fennel. Drizzle with extra virgin olive oil; add freshly ground pepper and serve.

*The *Faba vulgaris* or broad bean has been consumed in the Mediterranean basin for thousands of years. The many popular cultivars available are generally divided into short or long pod varieties. In either case the enclosed beans are best consumed when they are tiny and still quite green. When larger and more mature, they develop tough outer skins that must be removed.

**Widely used in the cuisines of many Mediterranean countries, the *Foeniculum vulgarae* grows freely in the arid soil which is inhospitable to many other plants. Its feathery leaves add a vaguely anise-like flavor to many dishes, while the tiny fruits (often mistaken for seeds) are most frequently used in breads and sweets.

***A cured pork product produced primarily in the Alto Adige region, this relatively lean *salume* is made from the posterior portion of the haunch, treated with a mixture of salt and spices. The subsequent smoking and aging phases are largely responsible for its characteristic flavor.

Shrimp "flowers" with green tangerine oil

Serves 4

16 red shrimp such as those from Mazara del Vallo
(shelled and deveined)
4 large Swiss chard leaves
1/2 yellow bell pepper
4 teaspoons Beluga caviar
80 g (2 3/4 oz) olive oil infused with green
Marzullo tangerines* (see page 106)
juice of 2 lemons
kosher salt
black peppercorns

Blanch the Swiss chard leaves in boiling salted water for 1 minute. Transfer to ice water to stop the cooking process, drain and arrange the leaves without overlapping on a sheet of plastic wrap. Place two raw shrimp tails on each leaf of Swiss chard, top with a strip of yellow bell pepper of the same length and then two more shrimp tails. With the aid of the plastic wrap, roll up the leaf so that it resembles a small sausage. Repeat the process with the other three Swiss chard leaves and the remaining shrimp and yellow bell pepper. Place these packets in the freezer for 1 hour, then remove them, eliminate the plastic wrap and slice each packet crosswise creating thin slices.

Presentation Arrange the slices in a circular pattern on each plate to resemble the petals of a flower. Garnish with a dollop of caviar and drizzle with an emulsion of the tangerine infused oil and lemon juice. Dust with kosher salt and freshly crushed black pepper.

* Marzullo tangerines, one of the many special citrus fruits grown in Sicily, are largely cultivated in the province of Palermo. They ripen in March and are often used in this period to create an aromatically infused extra virgin olive oil.

Pâté of smoked tuna and swordfish with onion "jam"

Serves 10

100 g (3 1/2 oz) smoked swordfish
100 g (3 1/2 oz) smoked tuna
100 g (3 1/2 oz) unsalted butter
juice of 1/2 lemon
10 g (1/3 oz) chopped onion
2 dl (scant 1 cup) whipping cream
additional ultra-thin slices of both types of fish for lining the terrines

Onion "jam"
1 kg (2 1/4 lbs) red onions, julienned
125 g (scant 4 1/2 oz) granulated sugar
125 g (scant 4 1/2 oz) unsalted butter
1 dl (scant 1/2 cup) red wine
1 dl (scant 1/2 cup) red wine vinegar

toast points

Patè Place the softened butter in the bowl of a mixer, add the two types of smoked fish (previously pressed through a sieve), the lemon juice and the chopped onion. Blend the ingredients at low speed for 20 minutes. Whip the cream and gently fold it into the above mixture.
Line two terrines (35 x 7 x 6 cm - 14 x 3 x 2 1/2 inches) with plastic wrap and then with the alternating slices of the two types of smoked fish. Fill them with the above mixture, close with the overhanging slices of fish and the plastic wrap and refrigerate for at least 5 hours.

Onion "jam" In a large sauté pan melt the butter over medium heat. Add the julienned onions, reduce the flame and cook them for 1 hour, stirring frequently so that they do not burn. Add the sugar, raise the heat and allow it to caramelize along with the onions. They should take on deep brown color. Deglaze with the wine and vinegar and reduce for an additional 10 minutes.

Presentation Just before serving, unmold the terrines. Place a slice in the center of each serving plate and serve with toast points and a generous spoonful of the onion "jam."

A "tin" of anchovies, eggplant and apples in black oil

Serves 8

24 fresh anchovy fillets
100 g (3 1/2 oz) extra virgin olive oil
juice of 2 lemons
salt, pepper

"Tin"
1 large eggplant
2 Granny Smith apples
1 teaspoon chopped fresh thyme
1/2 teaspoon chopped rosemary
50 g (1 3/4 oz) raisins
100 g (3 1/2 oz) Moscato passito di Pantelleria*
100 g (3 1/2 oz) extra virgin olive oil
salt, pepper

Black oil (see page 106)

Equipment
8 bottomless rectangular stainless steel forms that resemble anchovy tins (9 x 5 x 3 cm – 3 1/2 x 2 x 1 inch)

Soak the raisins in the wine overnight. Prepare the black oil as indicated on page 106. Marinate the anchovies in an emulsion of the extra virgin olive oil, lemon juice, salt and pepper.

Peel the eggplant and the apples and reduce both to a 1 cm (1/3 inch) dice. Briefly sauté them in the extra virgin olive oil without allowing them to color. Add the thyme, the rosemary, the drained raisins and continue cooking for 5 minutes over a low flame. Salt and pepper to taste and complete cooking in a preheated 150° C (302° F) oven for 20 minutes.

Presentation Place a "tin" in the center of each serving plate, fill it with the eggplant mixture and top with 3 marinated anchovy fillets. Carefully remove the form; decorate with the "black" oil.

*A sweet wine produced on the island of Pantelleria from zibibbo grapes that have been allowed to dry under particular climactic conditions.

Terrine of duck foie gras with apples and golden raisins

Serves 10

1 kg (2 1/4 lbs) duck foie gras
100 g (3 1/2 oz) golden raisins
50 g (1 3/4 oz) pine nuts
100 g (3 1/2 oz) chopped almonds
50 g (1 3/4 oz) chopped pistachio nuts
caramelized zest of 1/2 orange
1/2 tablespoon rum
1/2 tablespoon Cointreau
salt, pepper

Port gelatin
1/2 lt (2 cups) port
2 1/2 gelatin leaves

Garnish
1/2 apple
50 g (1 3/4 oz) toasted hazelnuts

Line a rectangular terrine (35 x 7 x 6 cm - 14 x 3 x 2 1/2 inches) with plastic wrap leaving enough excess to cover the top once the mold has been filled. Cut the duck foie gras into 1/2 cm (1/8 inch) slices and briefly sauté them in a non-stick pan without any seasoning (they should remain rare). Arrange a layer of foie gras slices in the bottom of the terrine. In a food processor finely chop the golden raisins, pine nuts, almonds, pistachio nuts and orange zest and blend with the rum and Cointreau. Remove the mixture, salt and pepper to taste and form it into a cylinder whose length is equal to that of the terrine. Position the cylinder on top of the foie gras slices, cover with additional foie gras (filling the terrine) and fold over the excess plastic wrap to completely enclose the foie gras. Top with a weight and refrigerate for 24 hours.

The following day, prepare the port gelatin by reducing the port over medium heat to 1/4 of its original volume. Add the gelatin leaves (previously softened in cold water, the excess pressed out). Remove the terrine from the refrigerator and unmold it. Smooth all of its surfaces with a spatula and coat it with the port gelatin. Return to the refrigerator to allow the gelatin to set. (Should the gelatin fail to completely cover the terrine, repeat the process).

Presentation Just prior to serving, slice the terrine (using a hot knife facilitates the process) and place a portion in the center of each plate. Garnish with the julienned apple (unpeeled) and sprinkle with the chopped, toasted hazelnuts. Serve with warm toast points.

Tiny squid with orange zest

Serves 4

500 g (approx. 1 lb) tiny squid, cleaned
3 tablespoons extra virgin olive oil
zest of 1 orange, julienned
juice of 2 oranges
salt, white pepper

Garnish
a few sprigs of fresh mint
orange zest, julienned

Slice the tiny squid crosswise to form rings. Heat the oil in a sauté pan and when quite hot add the squid and toss briefly (30 seconds). Salt and pepper to taste. Add the julienned orange zest, mix until just combined and remove from heat. Transfer the squid to heated serving plates and reserve. Add the orange juice to the sauté pan and reduce to a syrup-like consistency.

Presentation Nap the squid with the orange sauce; decorate with strips of orange zest and sprigs of mint.

Eggplant flan with Ragusano cheese sauce and a tomato emulsion

Serves 10

4 eggplants
100 g (3 1/2 oz) baby greens
(borage, Swiss chard, endive, etc.)
2 zucchini
1 onion
100 g (3 1/2 oz) tomatoes
 a few sprigs of flat-leaf parsley
100 g (3 1/2 oz) grated *Parmigiano reggiano* cheese
2 buffalo milk mozzarella cheeses (100 g - 3 1/2 oz total)
2 eggs
extra virgin olive oil
butter and breadcrumbs for coating the molds
salt, pepper

Tomato emulsion
500 g (1 lb) tomato sauce (see p. 108)
6 tablespoons extra virgin olive oil
20 g (scant 3/4 oz) chopped basil

Cheese sauce
1/2 lt (2 cups) milk
300 g (10 1/2 oz) grated *Ragusano* cheese*
50 g (1 3/4 oz) butter
2 egg yolks

Garnish
a few sprigs of fresh basil

Equipment
10 mininature timbale molds approximately 8 cm (3 1/4 inches) in diameter

Flan Peel and thinly slice two of the eggplants, arrange them on a lightly oiled baking sheet and bake in a preheated 180° C (356° F) oven for 30 minutes. Reserve. Peel and dice the remaining eggplants and sauté them with the roughly chopped greens, parsley, zucchini, onion and tomatoes in a little extra virgin olive oil for 8-10 minutes or just until softened. Transfer to a food processor and blend with the grated *Parmigiano reggiano*, the mozzarella and the eggs. Salt and pepper to taste.
Butter the molds, coat them with the breadcrumbs and eliminate the excess. Line the bottom and sides with the reserved eggplant slices and fill with the eggplant/cheese mixture. Bake in a preheated 200° C (392° F) oven for approximately 5 minutes.

Tomato emulsion Heat the tomato sauce and incorporate the cold extra virgin olive oil and the basil with an immersion blender. Keep warm over a double boiler.

Cheese sauce Bring the milk to a boil in a medium saucepan and allow it to cool to 80° C (176° F). Blend in the grated *Ragusano* cheese and then further bind the sauce by whisking in the butter and the egg yolks. Keep warm over a double boiler.

Presentation Unmold a flan in the center of each serving plate and spoon the tomato emulsion over one half and the cheese sauce over the other. Decorate with basil and serve immediately.

*One of the finest Sicilian cheeses, *Ragusano* is produced from whole cow's milk with a technique similar to that used for provolone. The large, rectangular forms may weigh from 6 to 12 kilos and present a smooth, thin, golden colored rind. The elastic pâte is delicately flavored in the younger specimens, but can become quite pronounced in the aged specimens which are often grated like *Parmigiano reggiano*.

Variations on the Pachino tomato

Serves 8

Bavarois
1 shallot
10 g (1/4 cup) fresh thyme
10 g (1/4 cup fresh oregano
400 g (14 oz) Pachino tomatoes: peeled, seeded and diced
4 sheets of gelatin
180 g (6 1/3 oz) whipped cream
1 tablespoon extra virgin olive oil
salt, pepper
20 g (2/3 oz) sun-dried tomatoes, finely diced

Tomato gelatin
200 g (7 oz) Pachino tomatoes
20 g (2/3 oz) granulated sugar
10 g (1/3 oz) cider vinegar
2 sheets of gelatin
salt, pepper

Tomatoes in green sauce
8 Pachino tomatoes peeled and halved
2 tablespoons green sauce (see p. 108)

Tiny tomato pizzas
18 discs of filo pastry (6 cm – 2 1/3 inches) in diameter
100 g (3 1/2 oz) Pachino tomatoes: peeled, sliced and diced
20 g (2/3 oz) hot pepper and vanilla infused oil (see p. 106)

Orange and tomato granita
250 g (8 3/4 oz) orange granita (see p. 109)
80 g (2 3/4 oz) diced Pachino tomatoes

Bavarois Sauté the chopped shallot in the extra virgin olive oil with the thyme and oregano. Add the tomatoes, salt and pepper to taste and continue cooking for 4 minutes. Add the gelatin (previously softened in cold water, the excess pressed out), allow it to dissolve completely and cool. When the mixture just begins to gel, gently incorporate the diced sun dried tomatoes and the whipped cream.Transfer to individual molds lined with plastic wrap and refrigerate for 12 hours.

Tomato gelatin Purée the tomatoes in a food processor and pass them through a fine sieve. Heat the purée over a low flame, add the sugar, vinegar and the gelatin (previously softened in cold water, the excess pressed out). Salt and pepper to taste and transfer to individual molds lined with plastic wrap. Refrigerate for 8 hours.

Tiny tomato pizzas Place 4 discs of filo pastry on a parchment lined baking sheet, brush them with extra virgin olive oil or melted butter and top with another disc of pastry. Spread a spoonful of diced tomatoes on each and drizzle with the infused oil. Bake in a preheated 200° C (392° F) oven for 1 minute.

Presentation Position a small container of the orange granita on each serving plate and top with the diced tomatoes. Surround with small portions of the bavarois and the tomato gelatin, one of the tiny pizzas and a halved tomato topped with the green sauce.

*A particularly firm and flavorful variety of cherry tomato, cultivated predominantly in the Sicilian town of the same name.

Cuttlefish salad with red and white tomato gelatin

Serves 4

200 g (7 oz) cleaned cuttlefish
juice of 1 lemon
extra virgin olive oil
a few sprigs of fresh oregano

Red tomato gelatin
7 firm, ripe tomatoes
1/2 carrot
1 celery rib
peel of 1 zucchini
1/4 lt (1 cup) fish fumet (see page 107)
40 g (scant 1 1/2 oz) powdered gelatin
salt
hot red pepper

White tomato gelatin
3 sheets of gelatin
the liquid extracted from the tomatoes above

Garnish
white tomato gelatin
100 g (3 1/2 oz) cuttlefish sauce (see page 108)
extra virgin olive oil

Equipment
8 bottomless ring molds 10 cm (4-inches) in diameter

Cook the cuttlefish in boiling water for 4 minutes. Drain and julienne it; season with an emulsion of extra virgin olive oil, lemon juice and oregano. Cool and reserve.

Red gelatin Peel, quarter and seed the tomatoes. Salt them, then purée in a food processor. Transfer the purée to a fine mesh sieve set over a non-reactive bowl to drain; reserve the liquid (it will serve as the basis for the white tomato gelatin). Reduce the carrot, celery and zucchini peel to a very fine dice; blanch in boiling salted water for 2-3 minutes and then transfer to ice water to stop the cooking process. Drain and reserve.

Wrap the bottoms of the ring molds with plastic wrap, creating a base. In the meantime transfer the tomato pulp to a bowl along with the mixed vegetables.

Heat the fish fumet over a low flame, add the powdered gelatin and remove from heat at the first sign of boiling. Incorporate the tomato pulp and mixed vegetables. Salt and add hot red pepper to taste. Cool then distribute among the 8 ring molds creating an even layer of the mixture in the bottom of each. Refrigerate.

White gelatin Filter the reserved tomato liquid. Soften the leaves of gelatin in cold water, squeeze out the excess and add them to the tomato liquid. Bring it just to the boiling point then remove from heat. Transfer to a shallow container; refrigerate until set, then reduce it to a 1/2 cm (approx. 1/8 inch) dice.

Distribute the cuttlefish among 4 of the ring molds on top of the red gelatin layer. Take care not to fill them completely. Remove the gelatin layers from the remaining 4 molds and carefully place one on top of each layer of cuttlefish in the other molds.

Presentation Just before serving invert a gelatin in the center of each plate. Surround with the cubes of white gelatin, decorate with the filtered cuttlefish sauce and brush each with a little extra virgin olive oil.

Salt cod
and dentex salad

Serves 8

1 lt (1 quart) vegetable broth (see page 107)
250 g (8 3/4 oz) dentex fillets
250 g (8 3/4 oz) salt cod, soaked and boiled
2 egg whites
50 g (1 3/4 oz) mayonnaise
500 g (1 lb) firm, ripe tomatoes: peeled, seeded and diced
20 g (3/4 oz) pitted olives
8 basil leaves
300 g (10 1/2 oz) tiny green beans cooked until crisp-tender
salt, pepper

Vinaigrette
100 g (3 1/2 oz) traditional balsamic vinegar of Modena reduced by 75%
1 dl (scant 1/2 cup) extra virgin olive oil
salt, pepper

Garnish
8 orange *tuiles* (see page 109)
orange zest

Equipment
a bottomless ring mold 12 cm (4 3/4 inches) in diameter
a bottomless ring mold 8 cm (3 inches) in diameter

Vinaigrette Emulsify the reduced balsamic vinegar with the extra virgin olive oil; salt and pepper to taste.

Cook the dentex fillets in the vegetable broth, drain, cool, break them into bite-sized pieces and reserve them. Beat the egg whites until they form soft peaks and gently incorporate them into the mayonnaise. Combine the cooked salt cod (similarly reduced to bite-sized pieces) with the dentex, add the mayonnaise and mix gently.

Dress the tomatoes with the finely diced olives, chopped basil, salt and pepper.

Dress the green beans with 80% of the vinaigrette.

Presentation   With the aid of the larger metal ring, arrange a bed of the tomato mixture in the center of each plate. Remove the ring, top with the smaller ring and use it to create a layer of the dentex and cod salad. Remove the second ring, top with 1/4 of the green beans and finish with an orange *tuile*. Decorate with the remaining vinaigrette and julienned orange zest.

Sashimi selection
by the spoon

Serves 4

Spoon one
60 g (2 oz) raw tuna, julienned
10 g (1/3 oz) green marzullo tangerine infused extra virgin
olive oil (see pages 16 and 106)
8 g (1/4 oz) grated tuna *bottarga**
lemon juice
salt, pepper

Spoon two
60 g (2 oz) raw cuttlefish, cleaned and finely diced
pinch of ground star anise
extra virgin olive oil
lemon juice
salt, pepper

Spoon three
4 raw shrimp tails, shelled and deveined
10 g (2 tablespoons) orange vinaigrette (see page 106)
salt, pepper

Spoon four
4 raw scampi tails, shelled and deveined
Sevruga caviar
extra virgin olive oil
lemon juice
salt, pepper

Spoon five
60 g (2 oz) raw dentex, thinly sliced
8 g (1/4 oz) green sauce (see page 108)
10 dried cherry tomatoes
extra virgin olive oil
lemon juice
salt, pepper

Presentation Arrange five spoons on a rectangular plate, each containing one of the following preparations:

Spoon one: tuna seasoned with an emulsion of the green tangerine oil, lemon juice, salt and pepper, topped with grated *bottarga*

Spoon two: cuttlefish seasoned with an emulsion of extra virgin olive oil, lemon juice, star anise salt and pepper

Spoon three: shrimp seasoned with the orange vinaigrette, salt and pepper

Spoon four: scampi seasoned with an emulsion of extra virgin olive oil, lemon juice, salt and pepper, topped with Sevruga caviar

Spoon five: spread a little green sauce on each slice of dentex, roll it up, season with an emulsion of extra virgin olive oil, lemon juice, salt and pepper; decorate with chopped dried tomato.

*The dried, salted and pressed roe of grey mullet or tuna, *bottarga* is considered a delicacy. It is most often added to dishes in their final stages so that its distinctive flavor is not altered by any cooking process..

Mosaic of tuna and baby vegetables in an olive caper sauce

Serves 8

1 leek
1 red bell pepper
50 g (1 3/4 oz) tomatoes, peeled, seeded, halved and dehydrated in a 90° C (194° F) oven for 1 hour
50 g (1 3/4 oz) pitted black olives
1/2 eggplant
5 porcini mushroom caps
2 large carrots thinly sliced lengthwise and blanched
2 medium carrots peeled and trimmed to an even cylindrical shape
2 zucchini trimmed to an even cylindrical shape
5 dl (2 cups) water
400 g (14 oz) fresh tuna fillet
50 g (1 3/4 oz) fresh ginger

Gelatin
250 g fish fumet (see page 107)
3 sheets of gelatin
basil

Olive caper sauce
50 g (1 3/4 oz) capers rinsed of their brine
100 g (3 1/2 oz) pitted black olives
1 dl (scant 1/2 cup) extra virgin olive oil
15 g (1/2 oz) red wine vinegar

Garnish
1/2 tomato, finely diced

Gelatin Heat the fish fumet over a medium flame, add the gelatin (previously soaked in cold water, the excess pressed out) and the basil. Remove from heat and cool to room temperature.

Divide the red pepper in half, seed it and place it in a hot oven until the skin blackens and is easily removed. Cut it into strips and reserve.
Peel the eggplant and reduce to 1 cm (slightly less than 1/2 inch) slices. Brush them with olive oil and grill them on both sides. Transfer to paper towels to drain. Prepare the porcini mushrooms in the same manner.
Cook the medium sized carrots, the zucchini and the leek separately in boiling salted water (taking care that they do not remain too crisp). 5-6 minutes should suffice for the carrots, 2-3 minutes for the zucchini and 10 minutes for the leek. Drain all of the vegetables on paper towels. Bring the water to a boil with the vinegar and a little salt and poach the tuna fillet for 2 minutes. Drain and transfer to an ice bath to stop the cooking process (it should remain raw at the center). Peel the ginger root and reduce it to tiny rounds.

Line a terrine (35 x 7 x 6 cm - 14 x 3 x 2 1/2 inches) with plastic wrap and cover the bottom with the blanched carrot slices, overlapping them slightly. Begin filling the terrine by alternating layers (and colors) of a single type of vegetable with one of gelatin. The leek should be trimmed to the length of the terrine and inserted whole. When the terrine is nearly half full, insert the tuna fillet and top it with a layer of ginger. Continue alternating layers of vegetables and gelatin, finishing with another layer of blanched carrot slices. Top with a weight and refrigerate for 24 hours.

Olive caper sauce Place all of the ingredients in a food processor and purée. Refrigerate for 2 hours.

Presentation Remove the terrine from the mold and eliminate the plastic wrap. Place a slice on each plate and surround with the olive-caper sauce and diced tomatoes.

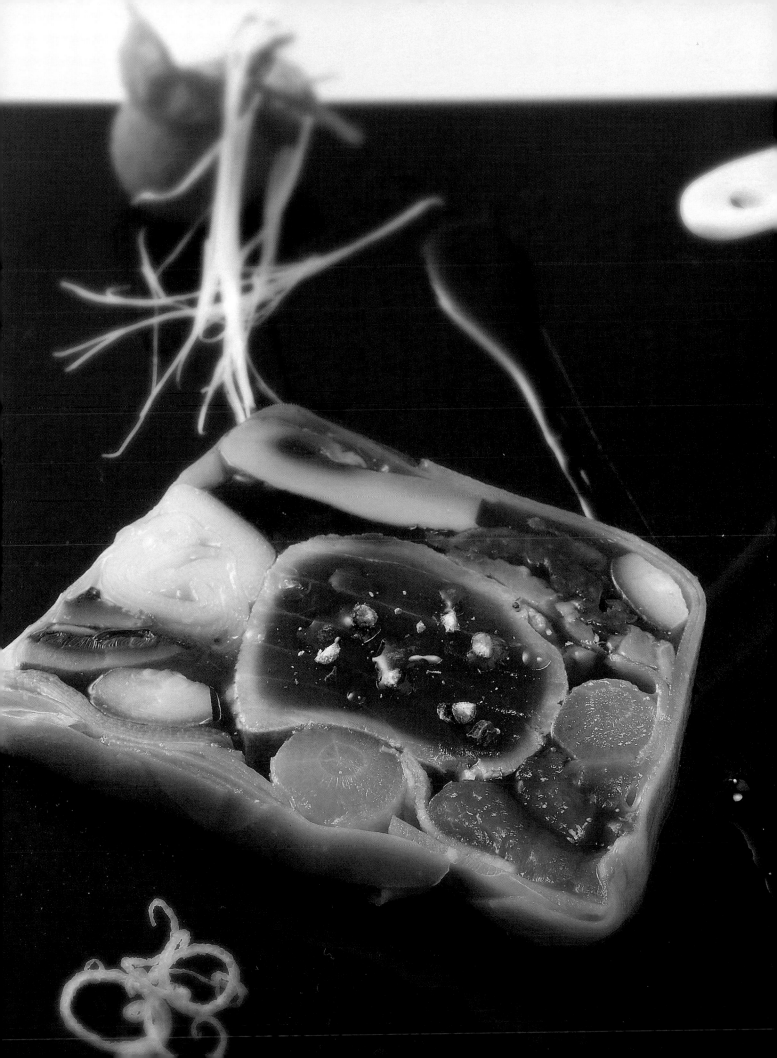

Shrimp croquettes with tomato sauce

Serves 4

Croquettes
200 g (7 oz) white bread (crust removed)
80 g (2 3/4 oz) milk
16 large shrimp
12 shrimp tails (shelled, deveined and chopped)
12 shrimp heads
2 dl (scant 1 cup) dry white wine
1 egg
50 g (1 3/4 oz) fine, dry breadcrumbs
extra virgin olive oil (for frying)

Tomato sauce
4 firm, ripe tomatoes
20 g (3/4 oz) mustard
dash of hot red pepper
1 dl (scant 1/2 cup) extra virgin olive oil
salt

Mixed herbs
1 clove of garlic
1/2 spring onion
10 g (1/4 cup) flat-leaf parsley
10 g (1/4 cup) fresh mint
10 g (1/4 cup) fresh rosemary
10 g (1/4 cup) fresh sage
salt, pepper

Tomato sauce Peel, quarter and seed the tomatoes. Salt them and set them in a colander to drain for 2 hours. Pat them dry with paper towels and purée them in a food processor along with the mustard, hot red pepper and extra virgin olive oil.

Croquettes Soak the bread in the milk, squeeze out the excess liquid and transfer the dampened bread to a non-reactive bowl.

Chop the garlic, onion and mixed herbs and sauté them in a few tablespoons of extra virgin olive oil. Add the liquid extracted from pressing the shrimp heads and the chopped shrimp tails. Mix well, pressing the solids with a fork so as to extract maximum flavor. Total cooking time should not exceed 2 minutes. Deglaze with the white wine, salt and pepper to taste and transfer to the bowl with the dampened bread. Mix well, cool then add the egg to bind the ingredients.

Shell and devein the 16 large shrimp and cover the tails with the mixture prepared above giving them the form of elongated croquettes. Dredge in the breadcrumbs and fry in extra virgin olive oil until just golden. Serve immediately with the tomato sauce.

Orange and shrimp salad with tuna bottarga

Serves 4

12 large shrimp
4 oranges
200 g (7 oz) extra virgin olive oil
2 shallots
12 shards of tuna bottarga*
(comprehensively 100 g or 3 1/2 oz)
freshly ground pepper

Garnish
1 small bunch of chives

Shell and devein the shrimp and drop them in boiling salted water for no more than 1 minute. Peel the oranges taking care to remove all traces of the bitter white pith. Liberate the sections from the dividing membranes.

Presentation Arrange orange sections in the center of each plate like the petals of a flower. Top with the shrimp and shallots (each cut crosswise into tiny rounds) and the shards of bottarga. Season with extra virgin olive oil, freshly ground pepper and a dusting of chopped chives. Decorate with a few whole stalks of chives and serve.

* See note on page 26.

Artichoke and ricotta terrine with herb sauce

Serves 6

Terrine
4 boiled artichoke hearts
7 g (1/4 oz) agar agar*
250 g (scant 9 oz) ricotta
1 dl (scant 1/2 cup) whipping cream
salt, pepper

Herb sauce
3 dl (1 1/3 cups) vegetable broth (see page 107)
25 g (1/2 cup) chives
25 g (1/2 cup) flat-leaf parsley
10 g (1/4 cup) basil
10 g (1/4 cup) arugula
10 g (1/4 cup) baby spinach leaves
10 g (1/3 oz) celery
50 cl (1/4 cup) heavy cream
salt, pepper

Terrine Pass the ricotta through a fine mesh sieve. Purée the artichoke hearts in a food processor, transfer the pulp to a clean kitchen towel and press well to remove all excess moisture. Blend the artichoke pulp into the ricotta. Whip the cream and incorporate the agar agar (dissolved separately in a little water and filtered through a fine sieve). Mix well and gently fold into the ricotta mixture. Salt and pepper to taste.

Line a rectangular terrine (35 x 7 x 6 cm - 14 x 3 x 2 1/2 inches) with plastic wrap leaving enough excess to cover the top once the mold has been filled. Fill with the artichoke and ricotta mixture, smooth the top, cover with the excess plastic wrap and refrigerate for 24 hours.

Herb sauce Place the broth in the work bowl of a food processor, add the herbs and vegetables and purée. Transfer to a small bowl; whisk in the heavy cream and salt and pepper to taste.

Presentation Nap each serving plate with the sauce, top with a slice of the terrine and decorate as you wish.

*Derived from seaweed, this substance functions like gelatin yet results in a smoother texture. Available in bars or flakes, it is odorless and has a remarkable capacity for absorbing liquids.

Tuna and scampi sashimi with basil-infused oil

Serves 4

400 g (14 oz) freshest fine quality tuna
8 scampi
1 tomato
16 fresh basil leaves
6 tablespoons basil-infused extra virgin olive oil (see p. 106)
juice of 1 lemon
kosher salt
freshly ground pepper

Reduce the tuna to a tartare by hand-chopping it with a very sharp knife. Shell and devein the scampi. On each rectangular serving plate, alternate a strip of the tuna with one created by the scampi, repeating twice. Salt and pepper to taste. Decorate the longer sides of each plate with strips of finely diced tomato and the basil. Just before serving, drizzle with an emulsion of the basil-infused oil and the lemon juice.

Rockfish soup with almond cous cous

Serves 6

1.5 kg (3 1/3 lbs) various types of fish from the rocky coastal area (scorpion fish, monkfish, John Dory, eel)
1 onion
2 cloves of garlic
1 dl (scant 1/2 cup) dry white wine
50 g (1 3/4 oz) tomato paste
1 celery rib
mixed chopped herbs (flat-leaf parsley, rosemary, wild fennel*)
1 bay leaf
pinch of saffron threads
5 tablespoons extra virgin olive oil
2 potatoes
salt, pepper

Cous cous
200 g (7 oz) cooked cous cous
200 g (7 oz) finely chopped blanched almonds
pinch of ground cinnamon

Garnish
dash of hot paprika
2 tablespoons pine nuts
2 tablespoons golden raisins
1 cinnamon stick
1 apple
a few sprigs of marjoram

Equipment
6 miniature savarin molds

Soup Carefully clean the fish, filleting the larger specimens and reserving several pieces. (They will be used to complete the dish).
Finely chop the onion and garlic and briefly sauté them in the extra virgin olive oil. Introduce the various types of fish, continue cooking for a few minutes and deglaze with the white wine. Allow it to evaporate almost entirely, add the tomato paste, the chopped celery, the herbs, the bay leaf and the saffron. Add 1 liter (1 quart) of cold water, simmer for 1 hour, pass through a fine-mesh sieve and salt and pepper to taste.
Divide the filtered broth into two equal portions. One will be used to cook the cous cous in the traditional manner. Bring the other portion of broth to a boil; add the potatoes cut into pieces and half of the reserved fish fillets. Cook for 30 minutes over medium heat. The soup should take on a more robust consistency.
Steam the other half of the reserved fish fillets for 2 minutes and reduce them to bite-sized portions.

Cous cous Cook the cous cous in the fish broth according to the instructions on page 109. When cooking is complete incorporate the almonds and the ground cinnamon.

Presentation Transfer the cous cous to oiled savarin molds. Unmold in the center of each serving plate. Accompany with the soup topped with the steamed fish. Decorate with bits of cinnamon stick, finely diced apple, sprigs of marjoram, golden raisins, pine nuts and a dusting of paprika.

* See note on page 14.

Salt cod gnocchi in onion cream with toasted pine nuts

Serves 8

Gnocchi

200 g (7 oz) salt cod previously soaked in several changes
of cold water and cooked in boiling water
150 g (5 1/2 oz) heavy cream
1 egg
30 g (1 oz) grated *Parmigiano reggiano* cheese
pinch of freshly grated nutmeg
300 g (10 1/2 oz) boiled potatoes (cooked in their jackets
in salted water)
100 g (3 1/2 oz) all-purpose flour
salt, pepper

Onion cream

2 tablespoons butter
300 g (10 1/2 oz) spring onions, julienned
1 medium zucchini
100 g tiny fresh fava beans*
mixed chopped herbs (basil, thyme, rosemary)
1/4 lt (1 cup) veal broth (see page 106)
1 dl (scant 1/2 cup) heavy cream
2 tablespoons extra virgin olive oil
salt, pepper

Sauce

3 firm, ripe tomatoes
50 g (1 3/4 oz) pitted black olives
40 g (scant 1 1/2 oz) toasted pine nuts
a few sprigs of mint
pinch of saffron threads
220 g (7 3/4 oz) veal broth (see page 106)
extra virgin olive oil

Garnish

a few sprigs of mint

Gnocchi Blend the cooked cod, cream, egg, grated
Parmigiano and nutmeg in a food processor until you have
obtained a frothy mixture. Peel the potatoes and pass them
through a ricer while still hot; add to the cod mixture; salt
and pepper to taste and incorporate the flour to form a
soft dough. Divide the dough into 6-8 sections and roll
each one out on a floured work surface to a long rope-like
form. Cut each into small pieces approximately 2 cm (3/4
inch) long.

Onion cream Heat the butter in a sauté pan, add the
onions and cook for 5 minutes. Add the diced zucchini, the
tiny fava beans, the mixed herbs, the broth and the cream.
Continue cooking for 15 minutes. Transfer to a food
processor and emulsify with the extra virgin olive oil. Salt
and pepper to taste.

Sauce Peel, quarter, seed the tomatoes and reduce them
to a medium dice. Sauté in extra virgin olive oil for 3
minutes. Add the julienned black olives, the roughly
chopped toasted pine nuts, the chopped mint, the saffron
threads and the broth. Continue cooking for 4 minutes.

Cook the gnocchi in boiling salted water and drain them as
soon as they rise to the surface. Transfer to the sauté pan
with the sauce and toss to coat.

Presentation Place a ladle of the onion cream in each
shallow serving bowl; top with a portion of the gnocchi
and decorate with a sprig of fresh mint.

* See note on page 14.

Cannolo of chocolate pasta with eggplant mousse and Ragusano cheese sauce

Serves 6

Pasta
200 g (7 oz) finely milled semolina flour
200 g (7 oz) all-purpose flour
4 whole eggs
4 egg yolks
50 g (1 3/4 oz) cocoa
10 g (2 teaspoons) salt
1 tablespoon extra virgin olive oil

Eggplant mousse
2 medium eggplants
1 kg (approx. 2 lbs) ricotta
50 g (1 3/4 oz) almond flour
25 g (scant 1 oz) breadcrumbs
25 g (scant 1 oz) grated *pecorino* cheese
rosemary
basil
flat-leaf parsley
thyme
extra virgin olive oil
salt, pepper

Cheese sauce
1/4 liter (1 cup) whole milk
400 g (14 oz) *Ragusano* cheese*
1 egg yolk

Garnish
50 g (1 3/4 oz) tomatoes
50 g (1 3/4 oz) finely ground pistachio nuts

Pasta Mound the sifted flours on your work surface and create a well in the center. In a bowl beat the eggs, egg yolks, salt and extra virgin olive oil to combine them and pour into the well. Begin drawing the flour over the egg mixture with your fingers, gradually amalgamating the liquid and dry ingredients. Add the cocoa and continue working the mixture until all of the ingredients are well combined. (Approximate kneading time: 15 minutes). The dough should eventually achieve a smooth, elastic texture. Gather it into a ball, enclose it in a damp cloth and allow it to rest in the refrigerator for 1 hour.

Mousse Peel and dice the eggplants. Heat a few tablespoons of olive oil in a sauté pan, add the eggplant and the chopped rosemary and basil. Cook over low heat for 10 minutes. Purée in a food processor and cool. Place the ricotta in a large bowl, add the eggplant purée, the almond flour, the breadcrumbs, the *pecorino* and the chopped parsley and thyme. Mix thoroughly (the mousse should be homogenous and compact); salt and pepper to taste.

Cheese sauce Grate the *Ragusano* cheese on the large holes of a box grater. Bring the milk to a boil, remove from heat and add the cheese whisking continuously. When the cheese has melted, incorporate the egg yolk to further bind the sauce. Place in the top of a double boiler and keep warm over barely simmering water.

Assembly Roll out the pasta to form a thin sheet. Cut out as many 5 cm (2-inch) squares as possible. Arrange a strip of filling down the center of each square and fold the pasta over it to create the traditional cannolo shape. Bake in a steam oven for 6 minutes. Alternatively, the pasta may be cooked in a couscousier. (Traditional oven baking will dry out the pasta.)

Presentation Nap each serving plate with the cheese sauce (remixed with an immersion blender just before using), top with 2 cannoli and garnish with diced tomatoes. Sprinkle with the finely ground pistachio nuts and serve immediately.

* See note on page 20.

Lasagna with sardines and wild fennel

Serves 4

4 (25 x 7 cm – 10 x 3 inch) sheets of fresh egg pasta
(see page 109)

Sauce
250 g (8 3/4 oz) scaled and eviscerated fresh sardines
10 g (1 tablespoon) chopped white onion
1 anchovy fillet preserved in oil
20 g (3/4 oz) raisins soaked in moscato passito di
Pantelleria wine*
15 g (1/2 oz) toasted pine nuts
50 g (1 3/4 oz) blanched wild fennel**
1 envelope (approx. 1 g) saffron powder
30 g (1 oz) tomato paste
2 dl (scant 1 cup) of the water used to blanch
the wild fennel
extra virgin olive oil
salt, pepper

Garnish
extra virgin olive oil infused with wild fennel
(see page 106)
1 tablespoon toasted breadcrumbs
1 teaspoon toasted pine nuts
a few sprigs of wild fennel

Sauce Sauté the chopped onion in extra virgin olive oil. Add the anchovy, breaking it up with a fork until it dissolves in the oil. Add the sardines (reserving 8 for completing the dish) and continue cooking for 2 minutes. Introduce the raisins (drained), pine nuts, chopped blanched fennel and the saffron powder (previously dissolved in a little warm water). Thoroughly combine these ingredients; add the tomato paste and the water reserved from blanching the fennel. Salt and pepper to taste and continue cooking over moderate heat for 6 minutes.

Assembly Briefly cook the pasta sheets in boiling salted water for 1 minute. Drain well and coat each sheet of pasta with the sauce. Arrange each sheet in individual oiled baking dishes in the following manner: hold the sheet of pasta by one of the short ends over the baking dish and lower it folding it in an S pattern - first in one direction and then in the opposite direction – making a total of 3 folds. Top each with 2 of the reserved sardines and nap with the sauce. Bake in a steam oven for 1 minute. (Alternatively the pasta may be cooked in a couscousier since traditional oven baking will result in pasta that is too dry).

Presentation Place a portion of lasagna in the center of each plate, drizzle with the fennel infused oil, dust with toasted bread crumbs, toasted pine nuts, a few sprigs of wild fennel and saffron threads. Top with one the reserved sardines (lightly sauteed) and serve.

* See note on page18.
** See note on page 14.

Lobster soup with "broken" spaghetti

Serves 6

240 g (8 1/2 oz) spaghetti

1 live lobster (approximately 600 g or 1 1/3 lbs)
1 lt (1 quart) water

1/2 clove of garlic
1/2 onion
50 g (1 3/4 oz) flat-leaf parsley
500 g (1 lb) tomato pulp
1 lt (1 quart) lobster fumet
2 dl (1 cup) lobster fumet
1/2 lt (2 cups) lobster fumet
extra virgin olive oil
salt, pepper

Garnish
50 g (1 3/4 oz) finely chopped almonds
a few sprigs of flat-leaf parsley
1/2 clove of garlic
pinch of hot red pepper

Kill the lobster with a net slice through the head. Working over a bowl to collect all of the liquid released from the carapace, remove as much meat as possible from the body and claws. Reserve the shells. Prepare the lobster fumet by bringing 1 lt (1 quart) of water to a boil. Add the reserved pieces of lobster shell and simmer for 10 minutes. Salt to taste.
Finely chop the garlic, the onion and the parsley. Sauté them in a little extra virgin olive oil in a heavy bottomed stockpot. Add the diced lobster meat and the reserved liquid collected from the shells without filtering it. Cook for 2 minutes; add the tomato pulp, 1 cup of lobster fumet and continue cooking for 15 minutes. Salt and pepper to taste. Add the remaining lobster fumet, bring to a boil and add the spaghetti broken into pieces. Cook for 6 minutes over high heat, stirring from time to time to insure that the pasta does not adhere to the bottom of the pan.

Presenation Serve the soup in heated bowls garnished with a mixture of the chopped almonds, parsley, raw garlic and a little hot red pepper.

Margherite with red shrimp coral and ginger

Serves 4

280 g (10 oz) fresh egg pasta such as margherite or pappardelle with ruffled borders

Coral sauce
12 red shrimp such as those from Mazara del Vallo
2 tablespoons extra virgin olive oil
pinch of hot red pepper
salt, pepper

1 tablespoon extra virgin olive oil
1/2 clove of garlic
2 tablespoons tomato sauce (see page 108)
1 dl (scant 1/2 cup) fish fumet (see page 107)
2 tablespoons coral sauce (see above)
5 g (1 teaspoon) white almond flour (i.e. milled from skinned almonds)

Garnish
20 g (3/4 oz) fresh ginger reduced to a fine julienne

Coral sauce In a cold sauté pan combine the oil, the shrimp tails (shelled, deveined and cut into small pieces), the liquid pressed from the shrimp heads, the hot red pepper, salt and pepper. Heat slightly. Just as soon as the liquid from the shrimp heads turns red, remove the pan from the flame, transfer its contents to a food processor and purée.

In a large sauté pan heat the extra virgin olive oil, add the finely chopped garlic, tomato sauce, fish fumet and bind with 2 tablespoons of the coral sauce.
In the meantime, cook the pasta in boiling salted water. Drain when still quite al dente and transfer to the sauté pan with the sauce. Toss; add nearly all of the remaining coral sauce and the almond flour, mixing well.

Presentation Place a portion of pasta on each serving plate, decorate with the julienned ginger and the remaining coral sauce.

Risotto with quail ragù and shards of Ragusano cheese

Serves 4

300 g (10 1/2 oz) *Carnaroli* rice
2 quail
100 g (3 1/2 oz) grated *Parmigiano reggiano* cheese
50 g (1 3/4 oz) extra virgin olive oil
40 g (scant 1 1/2 oz) chopped shallots
20 g (3/4 oz) lard
2 cloves of garlic
1 tablespoon fresh, chopped thyme
1 bay leaf
1 lt (1 quart) quail broth (see page 107)
salt, pepper

Garnish
100 g (3 1/2 oz) *Ragusano* cheese*
1 firm, ripe tomato peeled and diced
4 teaspoons traditional balsamic vinegar of Modena

Bone the quail and cut the meat into small pieces (reserving the bones and trimmings to prepare the quail broth). Heat a few tablespoons of extra virgin olive oil in a large saucepan, add the chopped shallots, the lard, the bay leaf and the two whole garlic cloves. Sauté until the shallots and garlic have just colored. Add the thyme and diced quail meat and mix well. Remove the remaining lard, the garlic cloves and the bay leaf.
Add the rice and mix well, coating it thoroughly. Toast the rice briefly and add a ladle of simmering quail broth. Continue cooking, adding broth from time to time as it is absorbed by the rice. When the rice is cooked, though still *al dente* (approximately 16-18 minutes), remove from heat, incorporate the *Parmigiano reggiano*, salt and pepper to taste and stir in a drizzle of extra virgin olive oil.

Presentation Arrange the rice on each serving plate in a stellar pattern. Drizzle with a teaspoon of balsamic vinegar, top with shards of *Ragusano* cheese and garnish with diced tomato.

*See note on page 20.

Open John Dory tortelli in a parsley and garlic sauce

Serves 8

Tortelli
Fresh egg pasta (see page 109)
250 g (scant 9 oz) fillets of John Dory (or monkfish)
1 lt (1 quart) fish fumet (see page 107)
5 strips blanched leeks (for tying the pasta bundles)

Parsley and garlic sauce
extra virgin olive oil
25 g (scant 1/4 cup flour)
250 cl (2 1/2 quarts) fish fumet (see page 107)
100 g (3 1/2 oz) flat-leaf parsley
2 cloves of garlic
pinch of hot red pepper
salt, pepper

Garnish
3 tomatoes, peeled, seeded and diced

Tortelli Divide the fish fillets into 20 g (scant 3/4 oz) portions and poach them in the fish fumet for 2 minutes. Roll out the pasta to form a thin sheet and cut out 32 4 cm (1 1/2 inch) squares. Cook them for 1 minute in abundant boiling salted water. Drain, refresh in cold water and lay them on clean, dry kitchen towels to drain completely. Place 1 piece of the poached fish fillet in the center of each pasta square and roll up (as though you were forming a cannolo). Use the strips of leek to close one end of each tortello. Just prior to serving, cook the tortelli by steaming them for 6 minutes.

Sauce Prepare a white roux by heating 1 tablespoon of extra virgin olive oil over medium heat and incorporating the flour, whisking to avoid forming lumps. Cook over medium heat just long enough to eliminate the raw taste of the flour then whisk in the fish fumet and continue cooking for 10 minutes. Transfer to a food processor and incorporate the parsley, garlic, hot red pepper and enough extra virgin olive oil to emulsify. Salt and pepper to taste.

Presenation Arrange 4 tortelli on each heated serving plate, creating a square pattern. Place the sauce in the center and garnish with the diced tomatoes.

Red shrimp
soup with basil pastina

Serves 6

Basil pastina

100 g (3 1/2 oz) finely milled semolina flour
100 g (3 1/2 oz) all-purpose flour
1 teaspoon salt
1 whole egg
4 egg yolks
1 tablespoon pesto (see page 108)

Soup

500 g (1 lb) large red shrimp such as those from Mazara
del Vallo
20 g (3/4 oz) white onion
1 clove of garlic
2 tablespoons flat-leaf parsley
250 g (8 3/4 oz) tomatoes, peeled and diced
1 lt (1 quart) fish fumet (see page 107)
extra virgin olive oil
salt

Garnish

50 g (1 3/4 oz) almonds
25 g (approx. 3/4 oz) pistachio nuts
1/2 clove of garlic
a few sprigs of flat-leaf parsley
pinch of hot red pepper

Pasta Combine the two types of flour and the salt on your work surface. Shape the flour into a mound and create a deep depression in the center. Break the egg into this depression, add the egg yolks, the pesto and beat lightly with a fork. Begin incorporating the surrounding flour a little at a time until the eggs are no longer liquid. Continue working the eggs and flour together until you have obtained a soft dough. Knead it until it achieves a smooth, homogenous texture. Enclose in a kitchen towel and refrigerate for 1 hour. Roll out the pasta with a machine or rolling pin. Cut to form tagliolini (long thin noodles 2-3 mm or 1/8 inch wide), then further cut these crosswise to form tiny squares.

Soup Heat a few tablespoons of extra virgin olive oil in a medium stockpot. Add the chopped onion, garlic and parsley and sauté briefly. Shell and devein the shrimp tails (reserve the heads) and cut them into small pieces. Press the heads in a sieve and reserve the liquid they emit. Add the shrimp tails and the liquid obtained from the heads. Raise the flame and cook for 2 minutes. Add the diced tomatoes and continue cooking for 1 minute. Add the fish fumet and bring to a boil. Salt to taste, add the pasta and cook very briefly or just until al dente.

Presentation Finely chop the almonds, pistachio nuts, garlic and parsley. Add to the soup just before serving along with a pinch of the hot red pepper.

Ravioli filled with chanterelle mushrooms in a balsamic vinegar sauce

Serves 4

Filling
120 g (4 1/4 oz) chanterelle mushrooms
50 g (1 3/4 oz) Savoy cabbage
10 g (1/3 oz) tender young celery leaves
10 g (1/3 oz) leek
1/2 clove of garlic
1 small piece fresh ginger
60 g (2 oz) pork fillet
20 g (3/4 oz) Colonnata lard (or similar herb-cured lard)
extra virgin olive oil
salt, pepper
hot red pepper

Pasta
200 g (7 oz) all-purpose flour
5 dl (2 1/4 cups) water
5 g (pinch) of salt

Sauce
50 g (1 3/4 oz) traditional balsamic vinegar of Modena
extra virgin olive oil

Garnish
1 tomato
a few sprigs of flat-leaf parsley

Filling Carefully clean the mushrooms removing all traces of soil. Finely dice them and sauté them in 1 tablespoon of extra virgin olive oil for approximately 5 minutes. Salt and pepper to taste; reserve 1/4 of the mushrooms. Blanch the cabbage leaves in boiling salted water. Drain and chop roughly. Heat a few tablespoons of extra virgin olive oil in a clean sauté pan, add the cabbage, the roughly chopped celery leaves the finely chopped leek and garlic. Salt and pepper to taste and continue cooking for 5 minutes over low heat. Add the finely chopped ginger, mix well and reserve. In a food processor, finely chop the pork fillet and the lard. Combine this with the sautéed vegetables and the greater part of the sautéed mushrooms. Mix well to create a smooth, homogenous filling. Refrigerate until ready to use.

Pasta Combine the flour and the salt on your work surface. Shape the flour into a mound and create a deep depression in the center. Pour in the water Begin incorporating the surrounding flour a little at a time until the water has been absorbed. Continue working the water and flour together until you have obtained a soft dough. Knead it until it achieves a smooth, homogenous texture. Enclose in a kitchen towel and refrigerate for 1 hour. Roll out the pasta with a machine or rolling pin to form a very thin sheet. Cut out as many 7 cm (2 3/4 inch) discs as possible. Place a small mound of filling in the center of each, dampen the inner edges with a little water and fold over the pasta forming crescent shapes. Press the edges to eliminate air pockets and insure that the seal is not compromised.

Heat a little extra virgin olive oil in a large sauté pan. Introduce the ravioli and allow them to brown on one side. Deglaze with a little water, cover and cook over a low flame for 3 minutes.

Sauce Heat the balsamic vinegar over a low flame, add the reserved mushrooms and toss until heated through (approximately 2 minutes).

Presentation Nap each serving plate with a little of the balsamic flavored mushrooms. Top with 6 ravioli (browned side up) arranged in a circular pattern. Nap these with the remaining balsamic-flavored mushrooms, decorate with sprigs of parsley and diced tomato.

Seafood ravioli with artichokes, cuttlefish and clam foam

Serves 4

Ravioli
200 g (7 oz) fresh egg pasta (see page 109)
300 g (10 1/2 oz) delicately flavored white fish
such as dentex or John Dory
3 dl (1 1/3 cups) heavy cream
1 egg
1 egg yolk
salt, pepper
pinch of hot red pepper

Sauce
2 artichokes
1 spring onion
2 dl (scant 1 cup) vegetable broth (see page 107)
juice of 1/2 lemon
extra virgin olive oil

Clam foam
500 g (approx. 1 lb) clams in their shells
2 dl (scant 1 cup) cooking liquid
obtained from opening the clams
1 dl (scant 1/2 cup) dry white wine
1 dl (scant 1/2 cup) heavy cream
30 g (1 oz) butter
pinch of hot red pepper

Garnish
300 g (10 1/2 oz) cuttlefish with their ink sacs
a few sprigs of marjoram
extra virgin olive oil

Ravioli Fillet the fish and carefully remove any tiny bones with tweezers. Transfer the fillets to a food processor and purée with the cream, egg yolk, eggs, salt, pepper and hot red pepper. When you have obtained a smooth, homogenous mixture, transfer it to a pastry bag and reserve in the refrigerator until ready to use.
Roll out the pasta dough, forming a very thin long rectangular sheet. Pipe eight mounds of filling at even intervals (these ravioli should be rather large). Brush the edges of the lower sheet of dough with a little water to improve the seal. Fold over the pasta and carefully press around the mounds of filling to eliminate air pockets. Cut out 8 rather large rectangular ravioli.

Sauce Remove the tough outer leaves from the artichokes and their spiny "chokes." Dice and transfer to a bowl of water acidulated with the lemon juice. Heat a little extra virgin olive oil in a sauté pan. Add the chopped onion and drained artichokes, sautéing briefly. Pour over the vegetable broth and continue cooking for 3 minutes over medium heat.

Clam foam Open the clams by placing them in a large covered sauté pan with 1 dl (scant 1/2 cup) of water over medium heat for a few minutes. Filter the cooking liquid and reserve it. (Use the shelled clams for another preparation.) Reduce the wine by half in a medium saucepan, add the clam liquid, the cream, the butter and the hot red pepper. Bring just to a boil and reserve warm.

Presentation Slice the cuttlefish into thin strips and briefly sauté them in a little extra virgin olive oil. Add their ink and continue cooking for no more than 2 minutes.
Cook the ravioli for approximately 3 minutes in boiling salted water. Drain and transfer to heated serving plates. Top with the artichoke sauce. Quickly mix the reserved clam sauce with an immersion blender until foamy and add a few tablespoons to each plate. Distribute strips of cuttlefish over the foam, garnish with fresh marjoram, drizzle with extra virgin olive oil and serve immediately.

Risotto with grilled blood oranges and moscato passito di Pantelleria sauce

Serves 4

280 g (scant 10 oz) *Carnaroli* rice
60 g (2 oz) unsalted butter
1/2 onion, chopped
2 dl (scant 1 cup) dry white wine
1 lt (1 quart) veal broth (see page 106)
80 g (2 3/4 oz) grated *Parmigiano reggiano* cheese
120 g (4 1/4 oz) foie gras butter (see below)

Foie gras butter
60 g (2 oz) unsalted butter
60 g (2 oz) pâté of foie gras

Moscato sauce
1/4 lt (1 cup) moscato passito di Pantelleria wine*
1/4 lt (1 cup) duck stock (see page 107)
30 g (1 oz) butter
salt, pepper

Garnish
12 grilled blood orange sections
20 g (3/4 oz) caramelized orange zest
10 g (1/3 oz) candied ginger (see page 108)

Foie gras butter Blend the butter and pâté in a food processor. Refrigerate until ready to use.

Moscato sauce Reduce the moscato by 75%, add the duck stock and further reduce by half. Whisk in the butter to bind the sauce; salt and pepper to taste.

Risotto Sauté the chopped onion in the butter and add the rice. Mix well to coat thoroughly. Briefly toast the rice, add the white wine and allow the alcohol to evaporate. Add a ladle of broth, adjust the heat to maintain an even simmer and cook the rice (adding broth from time to time as it is absorbed) for approximately 16-18 minutes. Remove from heat; fold in the grated *Parmigiano*, and foie gras butter.

Presentation Place a portion of the risotto in each serving plate, top with a few sections of the warm grilled blood oranges, decorate with the orange zest and ginger; drizzle with the moscato sauce.

* See note on page 18.

Tagliolini with Trapani pesto, potatoes and fish tempura

Serves 4

280 g (10 oz) tagliolini
20 g (3/4 oz) ground almonds

Trapani pesto
300 g (10 1/2 oz) tomatoes, peeled, seeded and diced
2 tablespoons extra virgin olive oil
50 g (1 3/4 oz) grated *Parmigiano reggiano* cheese
30 g (1 oz) toasted pine nuts
10 basil leaves
1 clove of garlic
salt, pepper

Potato nests
2 medium potatoes
extra virgin olive oil for frying

Basil infused oil
2 dl (scant 1 cup) extra virgin olive oil
1 small bunch basil

Fish tempura
200 g (7 oz) various types of fish fillets, diced
water
all-purpose flour
1 egg
soybean oil for frying

Garnish
fried basil leaves (see page 108)
extra virgin olive oil for frying

Equipment
long handled nesting, wire baskets for potato nests

Trapani pesto Place the tomatoes in a non-reactive bowl, mash them with a fork and season with extra virgin olive oil, grated *Parmigiano reggiano* cheese, toasted pine nuts, chopped basil, chopped garlic, salt and pepper. Mix well and allow to rest for 1 hour.

Potato nests Peel the potatoes and slice them to a 2 mm thickness on a mandoline. Place overlapping slices in the nesting baskets and deep fry creating 4 potato nests.

Basil infused oil Purée the basil leaves with the extra virgin olive oil. Pass through a fine-mesh sieve. The resulting oil should appear quite green.

Fish tempura Prepare a light batter by combining the water, flour and egg. Coat each cube of fish and fry in the hot soybean oil. Reserve warm.

Tagliolini Cook the tagliolini in abundant boiling, salted water until *al dente*. Drain and transfer to the bowl with the Trapani pesto. Add the ground walnuts and mix well.

Presentation Place a portion of the tagliolini in the center of each plate. Accompany with the potato nests filled with the fish tempura and decorate with the basil oil and fried basil leaves.

Timbale of tagliolini with red mullet and wild fennel

Serves 8

320 g (11 1/4 oz) tagliolini

1/2 onion
10 g (1/3 oz) flat-leaf parsley
2 anchovy fillets preserved in oil
200 g (7 oz) red mullet fillets
50 g (1 3/4 oz) wild fennel*
50 g (1 3/4 oz) raisins
50 g (1 3/4 oz) pine nuts
1/2 envelope saffron powder
extra virgin olive oil
50 g (1 3/4 oz) fine dry breadcrumbs
salt, pepper

Sauce
250 g (scant 9 oz) tomato sauce (see page 108)
50 g (1 3/4 oz) wild fennel*

Equipment
8 miniature timbale molds (8 cm – approx. 3 inches in diameter)

Cook the tagliolini in abundant boiling salted water, draining them while they are still quite *al dente* and reserving the cooking water.

Sauté the chopped onion, parsley and the anchovy fillets in a little extra virgin olive oil. When the anchovies have disintegrated add the mullet fillets and cook them for 3 minutes. Add the chopped wild fennel (reserving a few sprigs for garnishing), raisins, pine nuts and saffron powder. Continue cooking for 2 minutes. Add 3 ladles of the boiling salted water used to cook the tagliolini and continue cooking for an additional 5 minutes. Salt and pepper to taste. Reserve warm.

Sauce Blend the tomato sauce with the wild fennel in a food processor. Reserve warm.

Assembly Slick the molds with extra virgin olive oil and coat them with a thin layer of breadcrumbs. Toss the tagliolini in the sauté pan with the mullet sauce. Divide the pasta among the molds and bake them in a preheated 215° C (419° F) oven for 8 minutes.

Presentation Nap each serving plate with the tomato sauce and invert a timbale in the center, add a mullet fillet, decorate with the reserved wild fennel and serve immediately.

* See note on page 14.

Tortelli *alla Norma* filled with tomato gelatin and stewed onions

Serves 4

48 discs of fresh egg pasta (4 cm - 1 1/2 inches in diameter) (see page 109)

Tomato gelatin
200 g peeled Pachino tomatoes*
10 g (1/3 oz) powdered unflavored gelatin
salt, pepper

Onions
100 g (3 1/2 oz) red onion
1 tablespoon mixed chopped herbs (sage, marjoram, rosemary)
2 tablespoons extra virgin olive oil
salt, pepper

Sauce
1 medium eggplant, peeled and diced
1 spring onion
100 g Pachino tomatoes
green extra virgin olive oil**
salt

Garnish
8 fried basil leaves (see page 108)
20 g (3/4 oz) salted ricotta

Tomato gelatin Purée the tomatoes in a food processor, salt and pepper to taste and pass through a sieve. Heat the tomato pulp in a small saucepan and add the gelatin. Mix well until completely dissolved. Transfer to a rimmed baking sheet and refrigerate for 2 hours. When the gelatin has completely solidified, dice it.

Onions Thinly slice the onions and sauté them with the chopped herbs in a little extra virgin olive oil over moderate heat for 20 minuets. Salt and pepper to taste.

Sauce Peel and dice the eggplant and sauté it in a few tablespoons of extra virgin olive oil with the chopped onion and the peeled, seeded and diced tomatoes for a total of 4 minutes. Salt to taste.

Tortelli Place a cube of gelatin and a tiny amount of the onion on half of the pasta discs. Cover with another disc, moisten the inner edges with a little water and press to seal. (It is important to work quickly to avoid softening the gelatin.) Cook the bite-sized tortelli in abundant boiling salted water for 2 minutes and drain well. Arrange six small circles of the sauce on each plate, top each with a single tortello, sprinkle with grated salted ricotta and decorate with fried basil leaves.

* See note on page 22.

** Sicilians commonly refer to extra virgin olive oil made from the *biancolilla* cultivar as "green" oil because of its vivid green color. If unavailable, it may be substituted with any fine quality extra virgin olive oil.

Risotto with *tenerumi* and mussels in a saffron sauce

Serves 4

400 g (14 oz) unshelled mussels
1 dl (scant 1/2 cup) water

Saffron sauce
2 tablespoons extra virgin olive oil
20 g (3/4 oz) white onion
1 clove of garlic
10 g (1/3 oz) flat-leaf parsley
1 anchovy preserved in oil
1 dl (scant 1/2 cup) of the reserved mussel cooking liquid
30 g (1 oz) heavy cream
pinch of saffron threads
salt, pepper

Tenerumi sauce
100 g (3 1/2 oz) tenerumi*
200 g (7 oz) peeled Sicilian zucchini**
50 g (1 3/4 oz) white onion
30 g (1 oz) chopped almonds
20 g (3/4 oz) pistachio nuts
20 g (3/4 oz) pine nuts
20 g (3/4 oz) extra virgin olive oil
pinch of hot red pepper
salt, pepper

Risotto
30 g (1 oz) white onion
3 tablespoons extra virgin olive oil
280 g (10 oz) *Carnaroli* rice
1/2 the *tenerumi* sauce (see above)
100 g (3 1/2 oz) grated *caciocavallo* cheese***
tenerumi broth (see procedure for *tenerumi* sauce)

Garnish
4 sheets of gold leaf
saffron threads

Wash and debeard the mussels eliminating any broken or open specimens. Place them in a large sauté pan with the water over high heat. Remove from heat as soon as they open, shell them and filter their cooking liquid. Reserve.

Saffron sauce Finely chop the onion, garlic and the parsley. Briefly sauté them in the extra virgin olive oil, add the anchovy and when it has disintegrated add a little of the reserved mussel liquid and continue cooking for 2 minutes. Thicken the sauce with the cream, add the saffron, salt and pepper. Reserve.

Tenerumi sauce Bring salted water to a boil in a medium stockpot. Add the *tenerumi*, the zucchini and the onion and cook for 15 minutes. Drain, reserving the broth to cook the risotto. Roughly chop half of the *tenerumi* and the zucchini and reserve. Purée the remaining *tenerumi* and zucchini with almonds, pistachio nuts, pine nuts, extra virgin olive oil and hot red pepper, creating a dense, light green sauce. Salt and pepper to taste.

Risotto Bring the reserved *tenerumi* broth to a boil. In a large saucepan, sauté the onion in the extra virgin olive oil. Add the rice and mix well, toasting it briefly. Add a ladle of the boiling broth and continue adding broth a little at a time as it is absorbed by the rice. (Total cooking time approximately 16-18 minutes). Add the reserved chopped *tenerumi* and zucchini midway through the cooking process. When the rice is nearly done, stir in a tablespoon of extra virgin olive oil, the grated *caciocavallo* cheese and the reserved mussels.

Presentation Arrange a square bed of rice in the center of each serving plate, surround with the two types of sauce, top with a sheet of gold leaf and decorate with saffron threads.

*The tenderest young leaves of the Sicilian zucchini plant.
** The island variety may be substituted with small, tender specimens of other varieites.
*** A robustly flavored cow's milk cheese widely produced throughout southern Italy.

Black and cardamom pappardelle in bottarga sauce with olive oil foam

Serves 6

Black pasta
200 g durum wheat flour
6 egg yolks
1 whole egg
1/2 tablespoon extra virgin olive oil
10 g (1/3 oz) cuttlefish ink
pinch of salt

Cardamom pasta
200 g all-purpose flour
5 ground cardamom seeds
6 egg yolks
1 whole egg
pinch of salt

Bottarga sauce
25 g (scant 1 oz) extra virgin olive oil
30 g (1 oz) sliced tuna *bottarga* (see note on page 26)
1/2 cup water used to cook the pasta
grated zest of 1 lime
pepper

Olive oil foam
1 dl (scant 1/2 cup) milk
1 dl (scant 1/2 cup) extra virgin olive oil
pinch of salt
pinch of hot red pepper

Garnish
240 g (8 1/2 oz) raw tuna in long, thin slices
thyme
extra virgin olive oil
grated lemon zest
salt, black peppercorns

Black pasta Combine the flour and the salt on your work surface. Shape the flour into a mound and create a deep depression in the center. Break the egg into this depression, add the egg yolks (beating lightly with a fork), the extra virgin olive oil and the cuttlefish ink. Begin incorporating the surrounding flour a little at a time until the eggs are no longer liquid. Continue working the liquid and dry ingredients together until you have obtained a soft dough. Knead it until it achieves a smooth, homogenous texture. Enclose in a kitchen towel and refrigerate for 2 hours. Roll out the pasta with a machine or rolling pin. Cut to form pappardelle (3 cm - 1 1/8 inches wide).

Cardamom pasta Combine the ground cardamom with the flour and proceed as above similarly cutting the finished dough into pappardelle.

Bottarga sauce Place the extra virgin olive oil in a large sauté pan, add the *bottarga* and slowly heat over a very low flame just enough to dissolve the *bottarga*. Add the water, the lime zest and the pepper, mixing well. Reserve.

Olive oil foam Bring the milk to a boil in a small saucepan. Cool it, add the extra virgin olive oil, salt and hot red pepper. Beat with an immersion blender until foamy. Reserve.

Cook the two types of pasta together in abundant boiling salted water until *al dente*. Drain and transfer to the sauté pan with the *bottarga* sauce. Mix well to coat.

Garnish Arrange each slice of tuna on a lightly oiled baking sheet in a compact, circular fashion creating individual "roses." Dust them with salt, pepper and thyme and bake in a preheated 180° C (356° C) oven for 1 minute.

Presentation Place a nest of the pasta in the center of each plate and surround with the olive oil foam. Top with a tuna "rose"; dust with grated lemon zest and freshly ground black pepper. Complete with a drizzle with extra virgin olive oil and serve immediately.

Fillet of red mullet in a vegetable crust with toasted pine nuts

Serves 4

8 fillets of red mullet (approximately 70 g   2 1/2 oz each)
extra virgin olive oil

Vegetable crust
1 yellow bell pepper
1 hot red pepper
2 celery ribs
1/2 leek
1 small bunch of flat-leaf parsley
salt, pepper

Garnish
1 carrot
1/2 green bell pepper
1 spring onion
50 g (1 3/4 oz) toasted pine nuts
1 dl (scant 1/2 cup) traditional balsamic vinegar of Modena
sea salt, black peppercorns

Mullet Reduce the vegetables to a very fine dice and mix with the chopped parsley, salt and pepper.
Carefully examine the mullet fillets, removing any tiny pin bones with tweezers. Brush the skin side with extra virgin olive oil and press the vegetable mixture on to the fish so that it adheres. Cook on a hot grill (vegetable crust side down) for 1 minute. Carefully turn the fish and complete cooking on the other side for 1 minute.

Garnish Reduce the vegetables to a fine julienne and reserve them in cold water to maintain their vivid color and crisp texture. Toast the pine nuts in a non-stick pan. Heat the balsamic vinegar in a small saucepan until reduced by half.

Presentation Place 2 mullet fillets in the center of each plate. Decorate with the balsamic vinegar reduction, the julienned vegetables, sea salt, freshly ground black pepper and the toasted pine nuts.

Olive and chick pea fritters with tepid lemon-marinated dentex

Serves 8

Dentex tartare
400 g (14 oz) dentex
juice of 3 lemons
zest of 1 lemon
5 tablespoons extra virgin olive oil
mortar ground fresh black pepper
kosher salt

Olive and chick pea fritters
1 lt (1 quart) water
50 g (1 3/4 oz) extra virgin olive oil
250 g (8 3/4 oz) chick pea flour
50 g (1 3/4 oz) pitted black olives, chopped
pinch of hot paprika
salt, pepper
extra virgin olive oil for frying

Garnish
8 cherry tomatoes
zest of 1 lemon
a few sprigs of chervil
reduction of traditional balsamic vinegar of Modena

Dentex tartare To prepare the tartare, carefully skin and fillet the fish, Check to see that all of the pin bones have been removed by running your fingers against the grain of the flesh (from the tail towards the head). With a very sharp knife, chop the fillets creating a medium dice and then continue chopping until the desired consistency is achieved. The correct texture can only be obtained by knife chopping as a food processor would quickly reduce the flesh to a purée.

Season the minced fish with the lemon juice, finely chopped lemon zest, extra virgin olive oil, salt and pepper. Cover and marinate for 1 hour in the refrigerator.

Fritters Mix the water, oil, salt, pepper and chick pea flour in a medium saucepan. Place over medium heat and cook, stirring frequently, for 30 minutes. Remove from heat, add the olives and paprika and pour onto a rimmed baking sheet. Smooth the top and cool completely. The mixture will solidify enabling you to cut out at least 8 round or square portions.
Just before serving, fry these in 160° C (320° F) extra virgin olive oil for 1 minute on each side.
Top the fritters with a layer of the marinated dentex and bake in a 200° C (392° F) oven for 1 minute.

Presentation Serve the fritters garnished with cherry tomatoes, lemons zest, chervil and a balsamic vinegar reduction.

Charlotte of potatoes and scampi in an herbed tomato sauce

Serves 4

16 scampi tails (shelled and deveined)

Tomato sauce
1 white onion
50 g (1 3/4 oz) extra virgin olive oil
400 g (14 oz) firm, ripe tomatoes peeled and seeded
small bunch of mixed herbs (flat-leaf parsley, basil, thyme, bay leaf)
1 dl (scant 1/2 cup) dry white wine
50 g (1 3/4 oz) fresh chervil
30 g (1 oz) granulated sugar
salt, pepper

Potato purée
400 g (14 oz) potatoes
50 g (1 3/4 oz) butter
50 g (1 3/4 oz) heavy cream
salt

Equipment
4 bottomless ring molds 10 cm (4 inches) in diameter

Tomato sauce Chop the onion and sauté it in the extra virgin olive oil. Add the diced tomatoes, the chopped mixed herbs, white wine and chervil (reserving a few sprigs for garnishing) and continue cooking for 20 minutes. Add the sugar; blend in a food processor; salt and pepper to taste. Reserve.

Potato purée Peel the potatoes and cook them in boiling water until tender. Pass them through a ricer, add the butter and the cream (heated slightly without allowing it to boil) and mix well. Salt to taste.

Scampi Steam the scampi tails for 2 minutes.

Presentation Using a ring mold to provide the form, create a disc of mashed potatoes on each serving plate [approximately 100 g (3 1/2 oz) per portion]. Top with 4 scampi, nap with the tomato sauce and decorate with the remaining chervil.

Rosemary-infused fillet of red mullet with eggplant caviar

Serves 4

Mullet
12 fillets of red mullet
10 g (1/3 oz) chopped rosemary
extra virgin olive oil
salt, pepper

Eggplant caviar
1 large eggplant
1/2 clove of garlic
10 g (1/3 oz) rosemary
20 g (scant 3/4 oz) mint
20 g (scant 3/4 oz) flat-leaf parsley
1 anchovy preserved in oil
6 capers, chopped
2 firm, ripe tomatoes
100 g (3 1/2 oz) extra virgin olive oil
salt, pepper

Garnish
20 g (scant 3/4 oz) powdered tuna *bottarga**
diced tomato
extra virgin olive oil
a few sprigs of basil
a few sprigs of chervil
basil-infused extra virgin olive oil (see page 106)

Equipment
4 bottomless ring molds 8 cm (approximately 3 inches)
in diameter

Eggplant caviar Place the whole eggplant directly on an oven rack and bake in a preheated 180° C (356° F) oven for 20 minutes. Remove from the oven and peel partially (leaving some of the skin intact will provide a nice note of color). Finely dice the eggplant and season with the finely chopped garlic, rosemary, mint, parsley, anchovy, capers, salt and pepper. Add a drizzle of extra virgin olive oil and the diced tomatoes (reserving a small portion for the garnish).

Mullet Carefully remove any pin bones from the mullet fillets with tweezers. Arrange the fillets on an oiled baking sheet, brush with oil and season with chopped rosemary, salt and pepper. Bake in a preheated 180° C (356° F) oven for 3 minutes.

Presentation With the aid of the ring mold, create a circular bed of eggplant caviar in the center of each serving plate. Fan 3 mullet fillets over the eggplant, dust with the *bottarga* and garnish with chervil. Accompany with diced tomato seasoned with basil-infused extra virgin olive oil.

* See note on page 26.

Fillet of dentex with creamed leeks and a sea urchin emulsion

Serves 4

4 dentex fillets (approximately 110 g – 4 oz each)
20 g (3/4 oz) all-purpose flour
extra virgin olive oil
salt, pepper

Creamed leeks
2 leeks
50 g (1 3/4 oz) butter
2 bay leaves
1 dl (scant 1/2 cup) heavy cream
salt, pepper

Sea urchin emulsion
flesh of 20 sea urchins
1 tablespoon extra virgin olive oil
10 g (1/3 oz) Beluga caviar

Garnish
chives

Scale the dentex fillets taking care that their skins remain intact and remove any remaining pin bones with tweezers. Coat the fillets with flour, shaking off the excess and sauté them (skin side down) over a medium flame in 2 tablespoons of extra virgin olive oil. Salt and pepper to taste; cover and continue cooking for 5 minutes. Reserve warm.

Creamed leeks Carefully wash the leeks removing all residual traces of soil and juelienne them. Sauté the leeks in the butter; add the bay leaves, salt and pepper and stir from time to time to insure that they do not adhere to the pan. After approximately 20 minutes, add the cream, continue cooking for an additional 10 minutes, cover and keep warm over a double boiler.

Sea urchin emulsion Purée the flesh of the sea urchins with the extra virgin olive oil. Strain, incorporate the caviar and refrigerate until ready to use.

Presentation Nap each serving plate with the sea urchin emulsion, top with a bed of the creamed leeks and then with a fish fillet (skin side up). Brush with a little extra virgin olive oil and garnish with the chives.

Amberjack
in a potato crust with
a zucchini flan

Serves 4

4 amberjack fillets (120 g – 4 1/4 oz each)
all-purpose flour
2 new potatoes
extra virgin olive oil
salt, pepper

Filling
4 slices white bread
grated zest of 1 lime
a few drops of lemon juice
mixed chopped herbs (mint, rosemary, flat-leaf parsley)
20 g (3/4 oz) grated *Parmigiano reggiano* cheese
extra virgin olive oil

Flan
3 zucchini
1/2 small onion
extra virgin olive oil
1 dl (scant 1/2 cup) milk
1 dl (scant 1/2 cup) heavy cream
1 egg white
hot red pepper
salt, pepper

Sauce
3 tablespoons orange marmalade
1 tablespoon orange blossom honey
40 cl (1 2/3 cups) red wine
juice of 1 lemon
juice of 1/2 orange
small amount mixed spices (cinnamon stick, cardamom, star anise, cumin)
3 black peppercorns

Garnish
black peppercorns
kosher salt

Equipment
4 (10 cm - 6 inch) ramekins

Filling In a food processor blend the bread (crusts removed) with the grated lime zest, a few drops of lemon juice, the herbs, the *Parmigiano reggiano* and just enough extra virgin olive oil to create a moist mixture. Reserve at room temperature until ready to use.

Flan Thinly slice the zucchini and the onion and sauté them in a little extra virgin olive oil. Salt and pepper to taste. Transfer the cooked vegetables to a food processor and purée with the milk, cream, egg white and hot red pepper. Divide among 4 buttered ramekins and bake in a preheated 175° C (347° F) oven for 10 minutes.

Sauce Heat the marmalade and the honey in a small saucepan and allow them to caramelize. Lower the flame, add the red wine, the citrus juices and the spices (taking care to press the cardamom pod to extract maximum flavor). Reduce by half (the sauce should take on a creamy consistency); remove the whole spices and keep warm.

Amberjack Make a lateral incision in each fish fillet creating a pocket and insert the prepared filling. Thinly slice the potatoes and use them to wrap the fillets. Mix the flour with a little salt and pepper and lightly coat the potato wrapping. Sauté in extra virgin olive oil, turning once. The potatoes should form a golden crust. Complete cooking in a preheated 160° C (320° F) oven for 4 minutes.

Presentation Nap each plate with the sauce, top with a fish fillet (halved to expose the filling) and garnish with the kosher salt and freshly ground pepper. Accompany with the zucchini flan.

Grilled squid on a bed of puréed vegetables with olive-caper sauce

Serves 4

4 squid (approximately 120 g – 4 1/2 oz each), cleaned
juice of 1 lemon
pinch of fresh oregano
salt, pepper

Vegetable purée
200 g (7 oz) peeled potatoes
100 g (3 1/2 oz) tiny green beans
peel of 1 zucchini
salt

Olive-caper sauce
100 g (3 1/2 oz) pitted black olives
20 g (3/4 oz) capers (rinsed of their brine)
1 anchovy fillet preserved in oil
extra virgin olive oil (just enough to emulsify the above ingredients)
pepper

Garnish
2 tomatoes
4 sprigs of basil
extra virgin olive oil
salt, pepper

Equipment
4 bottomless ring molds 8 cm (3 inches) in diameter

Squid Marinate the squid for at least 30 minutes in the lemon juice seasoned with oregano, salt and pepper then grill them. Keep warm.

Vegetable purée Boil the potatoes and pass them through a sieve. Repeat the process with the green beans and the zucchini peel. Combine the various purées, mix well, salt to taste and keep warm.

Olive-caper sauce Place all of the ingredients in a food processor and blend until you have achieved a smooth, homogenous sauce.

Garnish Peel, seed and dice the tomatoes. Season with extra virgin olive oil, chopped basil, salt and pepper.

Presentation With the aid of the ring molds, create a circular bed of the vegetable purée in the center of each plate, top with a grilled squid and surround with the olive-caper sauce and diced tomatoes.

Sea bass "roses" with lentils and an anchovy-caper sauce

Serves 4
480 g (17 oz) sea bass fillets
extra virgin olive oil
1 tablespoon butter
salt, pepper

Lentils
250 g (scant 9 oz) tiny lentils
2 1/2 lt (2 1/2 quarts) water
1 bay leaf
1/2 onion
1/2 carrot
1 celery rib
extra virgin olive oil
salt

Anchovy-caper sauce
100 g oil preserved anchovies
10 g (1/3 oz) capers (rinsed of their brine)
a few tablespoons of fish fumet (see page 107)
extra virgin olive oil
pinch of hot red pepper

Garnish
fried julienned leeks (see page 108)
fried julienned carrots (toss in flour just before frying)
extra virgin olive oil for frying

Equipment
4 single-portion circular molds with perforated bases to facilitate steam cooking

Lentils Bring the water to a boil with the diced vegetables and the bay leaf. Add the lentils (previously rinsed and picked over to remove any tiny stones) and simmer for 1 hour. Remove from heat; drizzle with extra virgin olive oil and salt to taste. Reserve warm.

Anchovy-caper sauce Process all of the ingredients in a food processor for 5 minutes. Pass through a sieve and reserve.

Butter the molds. Slice the fish fillets lengthwise creating strips approximately 3 cm (1 1/4 inches) wide. Arrange these in a circular pattern in the molds (creating a rose-like effect). Salt and pepper to taste and drizzle with extra virgin olive oil. Bake in a steam oven (or in a couscousier) for 5 minutes. (Traditional oven baking will dry out the fish).

Presentation Arrange a bed of lentils in the center of each plate, top with a sea bass "rose", (released it from its mold) and surround with the anchovy-caper sauce. Decorate with finely julienned, fried leeks and carrots.

Mupa rolls on crispy caponata with orange blossom honey and celery gelatin

Serves 4

Mupa rolls

8 *mupa** fillets
200 g (7 oz) rustic white bread (crusts removed)
100 g (3 1/2 oz) milk
100 g (3 1/2 oz) extra virgin olive oil
1/2 onion
200 g (7 oz) shelled and deveined shrimp
a few tablespoons of mixed chopped herbs (basil, sage, mint, rosemary, flat-leaf parsley)
4 medium shrimp tails, shelled and deveined
1 dl (scant 1/2 cup) dry white wine
salt, pepper

Caponata

extra virgin olive oil
1 onion
1 celery rib
1 peeled eggplant
2 tomatoes, peeled, seeded and diced
30 g (1 oz) capers (rinsed of their brine)
100 g (3 1/2 oz) pitted black olives
50 g (1 3/4 oz) pine nuts
30 g (1 oz) granulated sugar
2 tablespoons orange-blossom honey
2 tablespoons white wine vinegar
salt, pepper

Celery gelatin

2 dl (scant 1 cup) water
20 celery leaves (the paler leaves from the inner stalk are less bitter)
dash of salt
2 g agar agar**

Celery gelatin Bring the water and celery leaves to a boil for 2 minutes; add the salt, the agar agar, allow to cool, transfer to a shallow container and refrigerate until ready to use.

Caponata Heat the extra virgin olive oil over a high flame and briefly sauté the diced onion, celery, eggplant, tomatoes, capers, olives and pine nuts. Add the sugar and honey, allowing them to caramelize. Deglaze with the vinegar and continue cooking for 2 minutes. Salt and pepper to taste. Reserve warm.

Mupa rolls In a large bowl soak the bread in the milk for 1 hour in the refrigerator.
Heat half of the extra virgin olive oil in a sauté pan, add the chopped onion, the 200 g (7 oz) of shrimp and the chopped herbs. Use the back of a fork to break up the shrimp, mix well, deglaze with the white wine and allow it to evaporate. Salt and pepper to taste and transfer to the bowl with the dampened bread (the excess milk squeezed out and eliminated). Mix well and allow to rest for 1 hour. Gently flatten the fish fillets between two sheets of plastic wrap. Slightly overlap two fillets; spread them with a layer of the filling; top with one of the shrimp tails and roll up. Repeat with the remaining ingredients.
Place the *mupa* rolls on top of the caponata, cover the sauté pan and cook over a low flame for 5 minutes.

Presentation Arrange a bed of the caponata in the center of each plate, top with a *mupa* roll (sliced in half to expose the filling) and decorate with cubes of celery gelatin.,

*The Sicilian dialect term for the *Pagellus acarne*, the *mupa* is found throughout the Mediterranean. If unavailable, it may be substituted in this recipe by one of the many types of sea bream.

**See note on page 31.

Tuna "sausages"
with mint in hot sauce

Serves 4

Sausages
350 g (12 1/3 oz) tuna fillet in 12 thin slices
4 small tomatoes
20 mint leaves
1/2 onion
extra virgin olive oil
salt, pepper

Mixed vegetables
1 medium zucchini, diced
100 g (3 1/2 oz) cooked green beans, diced
50 g (1 3/4 oz) shelled and peeled fava beans*
extra virgin olive oil
salt, pepper

Hot sauce
150 g (5 1/3 oz) basic tomato sauce, whisked with a little
extra virgin olive oil (see page 108)
20 g (3/4 oz) white sesame seeds
20 g (3/4 oz) white wine vinegar
20 g (3/4 oz) granulated sugar
pinch of hot red pepper
1/2 carrot, finely diced
1/2 zucchini, finely diced
salt, pepper

Garnish
4 blanched strips of leeks
black oil (see page 106)
mint infused extra virgin olive oil (see page 106)
kosher salt

Equipment
12 wooden skewers

Mixed vegetables Sauté all of the vegetables in a little extra virgin olive oil for 1 minute over a high flame (they should remain crisp-tender). Salt and pepper to taste and keep warm.

Hot sauce Combine all of the ingredients in a non-reactive bowl and refrigerate for 1 hour.

Sausages Spread the tuna slices on your work surface. Top each with a few thinly sliced tomatoes, a mint leaf, a little diced onion, salt and pepper. Tightly roll up each slice of tuna (creating a sausage shape) and reserve in the refrigerator until ready to use.
Tie 3 wooden skewers together near their tops with a strip of leek. Repeat with the remaining skewers to create a total of four bundles.
Heat a large sauté pan over a high flame; brush the tuna sausages with oil and quickly brown them on all sides. The cooking time should not exceed 2-3 minutes in order to insure that the tuna remains somewhat rare.

Presentation Arrange a bed of mixed vegetables in the center of each plate and 3 tuna sausages around the perimeter. Spear each with one of the skewers and serve with the hot sauce on the side. Garnish with the black oil, the mint infused oil and a sprinkle of kosher salt.

*See note on page 14.

"Millefoglie" of artichokes, sea bass and scampi with orange vinaigrette

Serves 8

Vinaigrette
250 g (8 3/4 oz) extra virgin olive oil
125 g (scant 4 1/2 oz) freshly squeezed orange juice
50 g (1 3/4 oz) dry white wine
salt
pinch of hot red pepper
20 g (3/4 oz) chives

Artichoke mousse
7 boiled artichoke hearts
150 g (5 1/2 oz) whipped cream
juice of 3 lemons
salt, pepper

For the millefoglie
10 artichokes
juice of 1 lemon
100 g (3 1/2 oz) raw spinach
300 g (10 1/2 oz) sea bass fillets
1 cup dry white wine
10 scampi
1/2 lobster

Garnish
julienned orange zest
chives

Vinaigrette Emulsify the oil with the orange juice, white wine, salt and hot pepper. Blend in the chopped chives.

Artichoke mousse Pass the cooked artichoke hearts through a sieve. Transfer the pulp to a clean kitchen towel and squeeze to remove all residual moisture. Place the pulp in a bowl and delicately incorporate the whipped cream, lemon juice, salt and pepper.

Millefoglie Remove the tough outer leaves and spiny "choke" from the artichokes. Thinly slice them crosswise, creating rings. Cook in boiling, salted water acidulated with the lemon juice. Blanch the spinach leaves for 2 minutes in boiling, salted water; drain and julienne them. Poach the sea bass fillets for 5 minutes in simmering salted water to which you have added the white wine. Similarly poach the crustaceans in their shells (3 minutes for the scampi, 8 minutes for the lobster). Shell, devein and reserve.

Presentation In the center of each plate, layer the ingredients of the millefoglie in this order: mousse, artichoke ring, mousse, sea bass, mousse, spinach, artichoke ring, mousse, crustacean, mousse, artichoke ring. Season with the vinaigrette, decorate with strips of orange zest and chive stalks.

Sardine cakes with mint and pine nuts

Ventresca of swordfish with lemon-infused eggplant

Serves 6

Sardine cakes
400 g (14 oz) fresh sardines, skinned and filleted
100 g (3 1/2 oz) grated *pecorino* cheese
50 g (1 3/4 oz) raisins
30 g (1 oz) pine nuts
1 egg
1 clove of garlic
30 g (1 oz) chopped flat-leaf parsley
1/2 onion
salt, pepper
all-purpose flour
extra virgin olive oil for frying

Tomato sauce
1/2 onion
1 clove of garlic
extra virgin olive oil
1 kg (2 1/4 lbs) firm ripe tomatoes, peeled and seeded
1/2 lt (2 cups) water
pinch of hot red pepper
salt, pepper

Garnish
30 g (1 oz) fresh mint

Sardine cakes Combine the chopped sardines, grated *pecorino* cheese, raisins, pine nuts, egg, chopped garlic, parsley and onion, salt and pepper in a bowl. Blend well to obtain a smooth mixture. Form into balls, flatten slightly, dredge in the flour and fry in hot extra virgin olive oil.

Tomato sauce Sauté the chopped onion and garlic in a few tablespoons of extra virgin olive oil until just golden. Add the roughly chopped tomatoes and continue cooking for 30 minutes. Add the water a little at a time to compensate for the evaporating tomato liquid. Season with salt, pepper and hot red pepper to taste. Transfer the sardine cakes to the sauce and continue cooking over low heat for an additional 30 minutes.

Presentation Serve the sardine cakes in their sauce sprinkled with chopped fresh mint.

Serves 4

400 g (14 oz) ventresca* of swordfish
1 large eggplant

50 g (1 3/4 oz) fine dry breadcrumbs
3 tablespoons extra virgin olive oil
juice of 2 lemons
1 shallot
4 sprigs mint
10 g (1/3) oz flat-leaf parsley
50 g (1 3/4 oz) grated *Ragusano* cheese**
salt, pepper

Garnish
grated zest of 1 lemon

Dampen the breadcrumbs with 2 tablespoons of the olive oil and the lemon juice. Add the chopped shallot, mint, parsley, the grated *Ragusano* cheese, salt and pepper.

Divide the swordfish into 4 equal rectangular portions and make a transverse incision in the side of each, creating a pocket. Fill each with some of the seasoned breadcrumb mixture. Thinly slice the eggplant lengthwise (without peeling it) and use the slices to wrap the prepared swordfish. Sauté the packets over high heat in the remaining extra virgin olive oil, browning them on all sides. Complete cooking in a preheated 180° C (356° F) oven for 5 minutes.

Presentation Slice each swordfish packet crosswise, creating 4 slices of increasing thickness. Brush with a little extra virgin olive oil and dust with grated lemon zest.

*Traditionally, the choicest cut of tuna taken from the underbelly of the fish. The term is now often applied to the same cut of other large fish.

** See note on page 20.

Vegetable-stuffed scampi with almond foam

Serves 4

Scampi
16 scampi tails
40 g (scant 1 1/2 oz) Beluga caviar
extra virgin olive oil

Vegetables
1/2 potato
1/2 carrot
1/2 small leek
1/2 zucchini
50 g (1 3/4 oz) shelled fresh fava beans*
30 g (1 oz) shelled peas
sprig of rosemary
a few sprigs of marjoram

Almond foam
1/4 lt (1 cup) heavy cream
1 dl (scant 1/2 cup) dry white wine
1 dl (scant 1/2 cup) almond milk**
30 g (1 oz) almond flour
15 g (1/2 oz) unsalted butter
salt, pepper

Garnish
8 blanched, slivered almonds
extra virgin olive oil

Equipment
16 wooden skewers

Vegetables Finely dice the potato, carrot, leeks and zucchini. Mix with the fava beans and peas and blanch in boiling salted water. Transfer to an ice bath to stop the cooking process, drain and mix with the finely chopped herbs.

Scampi Shell and devein the scampi. Incise them lengthwise and fill them with the vegetable mixture. Thread each on a wooden skewer and reserve in the refrigerator until ready to use.

Almond foam Bring the cream to a boil with the wine and reduce by half. Incorporate the almond milk and continue boiling for 3 minutes. Thicken with the almond flour and the butter, salt and pepper to taste. Beat with an immersion blender just before serving.

Brush the scampi with extra virgin olive oil and grill them only on the side without the incision for 2 minutes.

Presentation Arrange 4 scampi on each serving plate. Accompany with the almond foam and garnish with the caviar, the slivered almonds and a few drops of extra virgin olive oil.

* See note on page 14.

** A condensed syrup or paste for making almond milk is available in many Italian supermarkets. A homemade version can be made by wrapping 1/2 pound of very fresh blanched almonds in muslin and soaking them in 5 cups of cold water for 1 hour. The bundle should then be pressed and repeatedly re-dipped until all of the essence of the nuts has passed into the water, which will turn cloudy. The addition of 1 cup of sugar dissolved in the water completes the process.

Ricotta and crustacean bundles in bitter cavuliceddi leaves

Serves 4

20 *cavuliceddi** leaves
8 shrimp
8 scampi
320 g (11 1/4 oz) ricotta
100 g (3 1/2 oz) heavy cream
extra virgin olive oil
small bunch of mixed herbs (rosemary, thyme, sage)
pinch of hot red pepper
salt, pepper

100 g (3 1/2 oz) cooked wild rice

Blanch the *cavuliceddi* leaves for 2 minutes in boiling salted water; drain, refresh and dry on paper towels. Shell, devein and hand chop the shrimp and scampi; refrigerate until ready to use. Place the ricotta, cream, salt, pepper and hot red pepper in a food processor and blend thoroughly. Transfer to a bowl and blend in the extra virgin olive oil, the finely chopped herbs and the crustaceans.
Arrange 5 slightly overlapping *cavuliceddi* leaves on your work surface, top with a heaping tablespoon of the filling. Fold over the leaves to close, forming a small bundle. Repeat with the remaining ingredients to form a total of 4 bundles. Steam them for 5 minutes.

Presentation Place a bed of rice on each plate, top with one of the bundles (cut in half to reveal its filling), brush with a extra virgin olive oil and serve.

*This typical Sicilian green of the *Brassica* family may be substituted with Swiss chard or spinach.

Ventresca of tuna in bottarga sauce with vegetables

Serves 4

400 g *ventresca** of tuna
2 tablespoons extra virgin olive oil
sea salt, pepper

Vegetables
1/2 leek
1 carrot
1/2 red bell pepper
peel of 2 zucchini
extra virgin olive oil
salt

Bottarga sauce
50 cl (2 cups) heavy cream
40 g (scant 1 1/2 oz) tuna *bottarga*, chopped
1 tablespoon unsalted butter
pinch of nutmeg
50 g veal stock (see page 107)
white pepper

Garnish
30 g (1 3/4 oz) shards of tuna *bottarga*

Divide the tuna into 4 equal rectangular portions. Brush with extra virgin olive oil and cook over high heat on a ridged grill pan, taking care that they remain rare at their centers. Sprinkle with sea salt and keep warm.

Vegetables Reduce the vegetables to a fine julienne and season them with extra virgin olive oil and salt.

Sauce Bring the cream just to a boil; remove from heat and add the *bottarga*, butter and nutmeg. Blend well and return to a low flame for 5 minutes. Add 50 g (1 3/4 oz) of the veal stock and continue cooking for another 5 minutes. Emulsify with an immersion blender, strain through a fine-mesh sieve and reserve warm.

Presentation Arrange a bed of the vegetables on each plate and top with the tuna cut into bite-sized portions. Sprinkle with shards of *bottarga* and surround with the *bottarga* sauce.

*See note on page 79.

Tournedos of tuna on a bed of onion "jam" in Marsala sauce

Serves 4

600 g (1 1/3 lbs) tuna fillets
4 slices of Colonnata lard or similar herb-cured lard
extra virgin olive oil
salt, freshly ground black pepper

Onion jam
1 kg (1 1/4 lbs) Tropea onions (or similar sweet, red onions)
125 g (scant 4 1/2 oz) unsalted butter
125 g (scant 4 1/2 oz) granulated sugar
1 dl (scant 1/2 cup) red wine
1 dl (scant 1/2 cup) white wine vinegar

Marsala sauce
150 g (5 1/3 oz) unsalted butter
1/2 onion
1/2 carrot
1/2 celery rib
a few sprigs of flat leaf-parsley
1 bottle Marsala
1 sprig rosemary
2 bay leaves
1 small piece cinnamon stick
1/2 lt (2 cups) veal stock (see page 107)
salt, pepper

Garnish
2 carrots
2 zucchini

Garnish Peel the carrots; wash the zucchini and scoop out twelve 1 cm (scant 1/2 inch) balls from each vegetable. Blanch them separately in boiling salted water (2 minutes for the carrots, 1 minute for the zucchini), drain and refresh in ice water so that they retain their crisp texture and vivid color.

Onion jam Thinly slice the onions and sauté them in the melted butter over medium to low heat for 1 hour. Add the sugar and allow it to caramelize. Deglaze with the wine and the vinegar and continue cooking for 10 minutes. Reserve warm.

Marsala sauce Melt 50 g (1 3/4 oz) of the butter in a sauté pan; add the julienned onion, carrot, celery and the chopped parsley and cook for 5 minutes. Deglaze with the Marsala and add the herbs and the cinnamon stick. Reduce by half; add the brown stock and further reduce by half. Strain the sauce through a sieve, salt and pepper to taste and bind with the remaining butter.

Tournedos Wrap each tuna fillet in a slice of lard. In a sauté pan slicked with a little extra virgin olive oil, brown the fillets on both sides over a high flame. (Their centers should remain rare). Salt and pepper to taste.

Presentation Arrange a bed of onion jam on each serving plate, top with a tuna fillet, glaze with the Marsala sauce and garnish with the prepared vegetables.

Cardoon-stuffed tournedos of beef with an artichoke and foie gras sauce

Serves 4

4 tournedos of beef
200 g (7 oz) cardoons*
4 spinach leaves
4 12 cm (5-inch) squares of caul**
20 g (3/4 oz) butter
1 tablespoon extra virgin olive oil
salt, pepper

Artichoke sauce
2 artichokes
20 g (3/4 oz) shallots
1 tablespoon extra virgin olive oil
2 dl (scant 1 cup) veal broth (see page 106)
1 tablespoon heavy cream
30 g (1 oz) foie gras
salt, pepper

Ratatouille
1 shallot
1/2 yellow bell pepper
1 zucchini
1/2 eggplant, peeled
a few sprigs of fresh thyme
1 firm ripe tomato, peeled and seeded
a few sprigs of flat-leaf parsley
extra virgin olive oil
salt, pepper

Garnish
fried leeks (see page 108)
fried tomato skins (see page 107)

Tournedos Blanch the cardoons (8 minutes) and the spinach leaves (1 minute) in boiling, salted water; drain and refresh. Trim the cardoon ribs to a length somewhat shorter than the tournedos; fit two together and wrap with the spinach leaves. Make an incision in the side of each tournedos, insert a cardoon bundle and wrap the tournedos in the caul to close; salt and pepper. Heat the butter and oil together in a sauté pan and brown the tournedos on both sides until the caul has completely dissolved.

Artichoke sauce Remove the tough outer leaves from the artichokes; quarter them and eliminate their spiny chokes. Briefly sauté them in extra virgin olive oil along with the chopped shallots. Add the broth, cream, salt and pepper and simmer for approximately 10 minutes over a low flame. Transfer to a food processor, add the foie gras cut into pieces and purée. Reserve warm.

Ratatouille Sauté the chopped shallot in extra virgin olive oil. Add the finely diced pepper, zucchini, eggplant and a pinch of thyme. Continue cooking over low heat for 5 minutes; salt and pepper to taste and add the chopped tomatoes. Complete cooking and dust with chopped parsley.

Presentation Nap each heated serving plate with the artichoke sauce. Halve each tournedos to reveal its stuffing and arrange over the sauce. Serve with a portion of the ratatouille and garnish with fried leeks and tomato skins.

*A vegetable cultivated primarily for its stalks, the cardoon is related to the artichoke though they do not resemble one another. Specimens are often bent and partially covered with earth to shield them from the light, a process that improves their tenderness.

**Caul is a net like membrane of pork fat that may be found at butcher shops specialized in fresh pork. Since it dissolves during cooking, it is excellent for protecting tender or fragile morsels without intruding on their flavor. It is inexpensive and freezes perfectly, so a quantity may be used over a period of time. To make it easier to work with, the caul may be soaked in lukewarm water for about 5 minutes until it becomes soft and loose. Rinse in several changes of water and use promptly.

Fillet of veal with eggplant mousse and Marsala sauce

Serves 4

480 g (approximately 1 lb) fillet of veal
4 small red onions, baked

Eggplant mousse
1 eggplant
1/2 small white onion
a few sprigs of flat-leaf parsley
pinch of hot red pepper
1 tablespoon ricotta
a few sprigs of mint
sprig of rosemary
extra virgin olive oil
salt, pepper

Marsala sauce
50 g (1 3/4 oz) unsalted butter
1/2 onion
1/2 carrot
1 celery rib
a few sprigs of flat-leaf parsley
10 g (1/3 oz) honey
2 dl (scant 1 cup) Marsala
2 dl (scant 1 cup) veal stock (see page 107)
salt, pepper

Onion jam
200 g (7 oz) Tropea onions (or similar sweet, red onions)
30 g (1 oz) granulated sugar
30 g (1 oz) unsalted butter
1/2 dl (scant 1/4 cup) red wine
1/2 dl (scant 1/4 cup) white wine vinegar

Eggplant mousse Roughly dice the eggplant and place it in a bowl of salted water for 30 minutes to purge it of its bitterness. Drain and transfer to boiling water for 15 minutes. In the meantime, sauté the chopped onion and parsley in a little extra virgin olive oil. Add the drained eggplant and continue cooking. Salt and pepper to taste and add a pinch of hot red pepper. Transfer to a bowl to cool, then add the ricotta, the chopped mint and rosemary and mix well with an immersion blender.

Marsala sauce Heat the butter in a sauté pan. Add the chopped onion, carrot, celery and parsley; cook for 5 minutes. In a small saucepan caramelize the honey, add the Marsala, mix well and transfer to the sauté pan with the vegetables. Reduce by half, add the veal stock and further reduce by half. Pass through a fine-mesh sieve, salt and pepper to taste and keep warm.

Onion jam Thinly slice the onions and sauté them in the butter over low heat for approximately1 hour. Add the sugar and raise the heat to allow it to caramelize. Deglaze with the red wine and vinegar, allowing both to evaporate. Continue cooking for 10 minutes and reserve warm.

Veal fillet Brown the fillet on all sides in extra virgin olive oil over high heat. Complete cooking a preheated 180° C (356° F) oven for 5 minutes. In the meantime, hollow out the baked onions and fill them with the eggplant mousse. Heat them through in a preheated 150° C (302° F) oven for 3 minutes.

Presentation Place a mousse-filled onion in the center of each plate, surround with slices of the veal napped with the onion jam and the Marsala sauce.

Rack of lamb with mint, tabbouleh and thyme ice

Serves 4

1 rack of lamb (approximately 1 kg – 2 1/4 lbs) trimmed
30 g (1 oz) fresh mint
extra virgin olive oil
salt, pepper

Tabbouleh
80 g (scant 3 oz) cous cous (see page 109)
10 g (1/3 oz) extra virgin olive oil
1/4 lt (1 cup) veal broth (see page 106)
10 g (1/3 oz) carrot
8 g (1/4 oz) sun-dried tomatoes
10 g (1/3 oz) fresh mint
1 tablespoon flat-leaf parsley
1 tablespoon rosemary
pinch of curry
pinch of hot red pepper
salt, pepper

Thyme ice
125 g (scant 4 1/2 oz) tap water
125 g (scant 4 1/2 oz) granulated sugar
30 g (1 oz) thyme
1 egg white
65 ml (1/4 cup) carbonated water
10 g (1/3 oz) lemon juice

Garnish
2 dl (scant 1 cup) reduced lamb stock (see page 107)
cooking juices from the roast
sprigs of thyme

Make a transverse incision along the thickest part of the rack of lamb and fill it with the mint. Brown the rack on all sides in a little extra virgin olive oil and complete cooking in a preheated 180° C (356° F) oven for 8 minutes. Salt and pepper to taste.

Tabbouleh Spread the cous cous on a ridged baking sheet; drizzle with the extra virgin olive oil and moisten with the boiling broth. Cover and allow to rest for 5 minutes. Uncover, fluff the grains with a fork and add the finely chopped carrot, tomatoes and herbs, the curry, the hot red pepper, salt and pepper.

Thyme ice Bring the tap water to a boil; add the sugar and the thyme and mix until the former has completely dissolved. Cool in the refrigerator for 2 hours before transferring to an ice cream machine along with the egg white, the carbonated water and the lemon juice. Process according to the manufacturer's instructions and reserve in the freezer until ready to use.

Presentation Arrange a bed of *tabbouleh* on each plate, top with a portion of the lamb (sliced just prior to serving); nap with the lamb stock and serve with the thyme ice. Finish with sprigs of fresh thyme.

Fillet of suckling pig in a crust of pistachio nuts with a bitter cocoa sauce

Serves 4

600 g (1 1/3 lbs) fillet of suckling pig
100 g (3 1/2 oz) ground pistachio nuts
2 tablespoons extra virgin olive oil
salt, pepper

Red wine sauce
2 lt (2 quarts) red wine
1/4 lt (1 cup) veal stock (see page 107)
1/2 cinnamon stick
100 g (3 1/2 oz) honey
100 g (3 1/2 oz) unsalted butter
salt, pepper

Cocoa sauce
50 g (1 3/4 oz) honey
1/4 lt (1 cup) veal stock (see page 107)
2 tablespoons red wine sauce (see above)
30 g (1 oz) cocoa
50 g (1 3/4 oz) unsalted butter
salt, pepper

Red wine sauce Reduce the red wine by 3/4, add the veal stock, the cinnamon stick and the honey. Whisk in the butter to achieve a syrupy consistency; salt and pepper to taste.

Cocoa sauce Caramelize the honey by heating it in a small saucepan until it takes on a deeper color. Add the veal stock and the red wine sauce. Simmer for 5 minutes and add the cocoa. Bind the sauce by whisking in the butter. Salt and pepper to taste.

Suckling pig fillet Heat 2 tablespoon of extra virgin olive oil in a large sauté pan and brown the fillet taking care that it remains rare internally. Remove from heat, dust with the ground pistachios and transfer to a preheated 160° C (320° F) oven for 4 minutes.

Presentation Arrange slices of the fillet on each plate; drizzle with the cocoa sauce and serve accompanied by a vegetable of your choice.

Crispy cannoli with ricotta cream and caramelized orange zest

Serves 10

Cannoli
250 g (9 oz) all-purpose flour
25 g (scant 1 oz) granulated sugar
pinch of ground cinnamon
pinch of cocoa
25 g (scant 1 oz) unsalted butter
1 dl (scant 1/2 cup) Marsala
lard for frying

Filling
500 g (1 lb) ricotta
175 g (6 oz) granulated sugar

Caramelized orange zest
100 g (3 1/2 oz) orange zest
100 g (3 1/2 oz) granulated sugar
150 g (5 1/3 oz) water
unsalted butter

Garnish
chocolate shavings
powdered sugar
orange blossoms

Equipment
10 cone shaped stainless steel forms

Cannoli Combine the flour, sugar, cinnamon and cocoa. Melt the butter in the top of a double boiler, allow it to cool and add it to the dry ingredients. Mix well and slowly add the Marsala. Continue mixing until you have obtained a smooth, homogenous dough. Enclose in plastic wrap and allow to rest in the refrigerator for 1 hour.

Roll out the dough forming a thin sheet. Cut out 10 triangles with an 8 cm (3 inch) base and 12 cm (4 3/4 inch) sides. Wrap the dough around the stainless steel forms and fry in batches in 160° C (320° F) lard until golden. Transfer to paper towels and, when cool, carefully remove the metal supports as the cannoli are quite delicate.

Filling Place the ricotta and sugar in a food processor and blend for 5 minutes. Pass through a fine mesh sieve and refrigerate for 1 hour.

Caramelized orange zest Reduce the orange zest to a fine julienne and transfer to a small saucepan with the water and sugar. Heat over a low flame until the water has completely evaporated. Transfer the strips of orange zest to a buttered baking sheet to cool.

Presentation Transfer the ricotta cream to a pastry bag with a ridged tip and fill the cannoli. Place one on each serving plate, garnish with the orange zest, chocolate shavings, powdered sugar and orange blossoms (when available).

Sicilian cassata "deconstructed"

Serves 4

Sponge cake
2 eggs
40 g (scant 1 1/2 oz) granulated sugar
40 g (scant 1 1/2 oz) all-purpose flour
cinnamon infused *rosolio**

Marzipan
40 g (scant 1 1/2 oz) pistachio flour
40 g (scant 1 1/2 oz) powdered sugar
pinch of salt
3 teaspoons water

Ricotta
200 g (7 oz) sheep's milk ricotta
40 g (scant 1 1/2 oz) granulated sugar

Icing
70 g (2 1/2 oz) powdered sugar
a few drops of lemon juice
just enough milk to provide a creamy consistency

Decoration
diced candied fruit
30 g (1 oz) cocoa
finely chopped pistachio nuts
1 cinnamon stick

Sponge cake Beat the eggs with the sugar until light. Add the flour, a little at a time, and continue beating until you have obtained a frothy batter. Line a rimmed, square (35 cm - 14 inch) baking sheet with parchment and fill with a very thin layer (1/2 cm – 1/8 inch) of the batter. Bake in a preheated 180° C (356° F) oven for 7 minutes. Remove from the oven and invert on a wire rack to cool.

Marzipan Mix all of the ingredients and allow the dough to rest for 1 hour at room temperature. Roll out the dough to a 2-3 mm (scant 1/8 inch) thickness and cut out four 2 x 3 cm (3/4 x 1-inch) rectangles.

Ricotta Combine the sugar and the ricotta; pass through a fine-mesh sieve and whip for 2 minutes to lighten. Transfer to a pastry bag with a fluted tip and reserve in the refrigerator until ready to use.

Icing Thoroughly combine all of the ingredients and transfer to a pastry bag with a very fine tip.

Presentation Center a small rectangle of marzipan on each plate. Surround it with the candied fruit. Cut the sponge cake into four 3 x 14 cm (1 x 5 1/2 inch) strips, dampen them with the rosolio, roll them up and dust with cocoa powder. Position in the center of each plate and surround with piped ricotta rosettes. Decorate with the prepared icing, dust with finely ground pistachio nuts and complete with pieces of cinnamon stick.

*A delicate cordial made from rose petals and sugar infused in alcohol. These basic ingredients are sometimes supplemented by other aromatic elements, such as the cinnamon above, in order to give the mixture a more complex aroma and flavor.

Citrus crème brulée

Serves 5

500 g (1 lb) heavy cream
100 g (3 1/2 oz) milk
8 egg yolks
80 g (scant 3 oz) granulated sugar
grated zest of 1 orange
grated zest of 2 bergamot oranges*
grated zest of 2 tangerines
grated zest of 1 grapefruit
brown sugar for sprinkling the top of each dessert

Equipment
20 small ramekins
kitchen torch

Combine the cream and the milk in a heavy-duty saucepan and heat over a low flame. In the meantime beat the egg yolks and sugar until light. Just as soon as the cream mixture comes to a boil, slowly pour it over the beaten eggs, whisking continuously. Divide the mixture into 4 equal parts and, while still hot, add one type of grated zest to each so as to obtain 4 differently flavored infusions (orange, bergamot, tangerine and grapefruit). Allow these to rest for 15 minutes then filter each through a fine-mesh sieve, maintaining the division of the various infusions. Distribute each type of cream among 5 small ramekins, for a total of 20 pots of cream. Arrange them in a baking pan so that you can distinguish among the various flavors and add just enough water to come half way up the sides of the forms. Cover tightly with foil and bake in a preheated 90-95° C (194-203° F) oven for 1 hour. Remove from the oven, cool and refrigerate for at least 3 hours.

Presentation Just before serving, sprinkle the surface of each pot of cream with brown sugar and caramelize with a kitchen torch. Arrange 1 portion of each type of flavored cream on each serving plate (so that each guest will receive 4 small differently flavored ramekins). Serve immediately.

*A fruit whose cultivation is confined almost entirely to the Italian region of Calabria, the *Citrus bergamina* resembles a pear-shaped orange. Its flesh is not edible, but its zest provides a fragrant oil that is candied for use in confectionary.

Tangerine gelatin with pink grapefruit marmalade

Serves 10

Tangerine gelatin
6 1/2 sheets of gelatin
1 lt (1 quart) tangerine juice
150 g (5 1/3 oz) granulated sugar

Sauce
100 g (3 1/2 oz) pink grapefruit marmalade
50 g (1 oz) white wine

Garnish
tangerine leaves

Equipment
10 single serving molds

Tangerine gelatin Soften the sheets of gelatin by immersing them in cold water. Heat the tangerine juice (taking care not to exceed 60° C (140° F) and add the sugar, stirring until it is completely dissolved. Squeeze the excess water from the sheets of gelatin and add to the tangerine juice. Stir until completely incorporated. Divide the tangerine mixture among 10 decorative molds and refrigerate for 6 hours.

Sauce Heat the grapefruit marmalade over a low flame and add the wine. Mix well and refrigerate.

Presentation Dip the molds in warm water up to their rims to facilitate extracting the gelatins. Invert each into a shallow bowl, add a few tablespoons of the sauce around the gelatins and decorate with tangerine leaves.

Note Don't be tempted to reduce the recipe as it will not work with smaller quantities of ingredients. Extra gelatins will keep in the refrigerator for 3-4 days if carefully covered with plastic wrap.

Orange foam with candied zest sauce

Serves 10

Orange foam
50 g (1 3/4 oz) milk
2 oranges
1/2 vanilla bean
6 g (1 sheet) gelatin
3 egg yolks
90 g (3 1/4 oz) granulated sugar
300 g (10 1/2 oz) whipping cream

Candied orange slices
3 oranges
100 g (3 1/2 oz) water
150 g (5 1/3 oz) white wine
200 g (7 oz) granulated sugar

Sauce
50 g (1 3/4 oz) granulated sugar
150 g (5 1/3 oz) freshly squeezed orange juice
julienned zest of 1 orange

Garnish
untreated orange blossoms and leaves

Equipment
10 semispherical stainless steel molds 10 cm (4 inches) in diameter

Candied orange slices Halve the oranges, place them cut-side down on your work surface and slice them very thinly with their zests to obtain half moon shaped slices. Transfer to a saucepan with the water, wine and sugar and bring to a boil. Simmer for 1 minute. Cool in the syrup then use the slices to line the molds, overlapping them slightly.

Orange foam Place the milk in a small saucepan. Add the grated zest of one of the oranges and the contents of the vanilla bean. Heat over a low flame, add the gelatin (previously softened in cold water, the excess pressed out) and remove from heat when it has completely dissolved. In the meantime, beat the egg yolks with the sugar until pale and light. Add the milk and continue beating. Incorporate the whipped cream and the two oranges (take care to remove all of the bitter white pith) cut into small pieces. Divide among the prepared molds and transfer to the refrigerator for 1 hour.

Sauce Caramelize the sugar over a low flame and as soon as it shows signs of boiling, slowly add the orange juice and the julienned orange zest. Simmer over moderate heat for 2 minutes, then cool.

Presentation Unmold the desserts in the center of each plate. Spoon the sauce around them and decorate with the orange blossoms and leaves.

Frozen cherry soufflés

Serves 8

Soufflés
50 g (1 3/4) oz butter
125 g (4 1/2 oz) pitted cherries
20 g (3/4 oz) kirsch
3 eggs
75 g (2 1/2 oz) granulated sugar
75 g (2 1/2 oz) powdered sugar
150 g (5 1/3 oz) whipping cream
brown sugar

Cherry sauce
100 g (3 1/2 oz) butter
200 g (7 oz) pitted cherries
60 g (2 oz) granulated sugar
50 g (1 3/4 oz) kirsch

Equipment
8 individual soufflé molds
kitchen torch

Soufflés Using aluminum foil, insert a collar into each soufflé mold, taking care that it extends a few centimeters (approximately 1 inch) above the border.
Melt the butter in a medium saucepan, add the cherries and cook for 5 minutes. Add the kirsch; carefully ignite to burn off the alcohol and cool.
Separate the eggs. Beat the yolks with the granulated sugar until light and the whites with the powdered sugar until they form soft peaks. Whip the cream. Delicately incorporate the cherries into the beaten egg yolks then fold in the whipped cream and the whites taking care not to deflate them.
Fill each soufflé mold to the border of the foil collars and refrigerate for 8 hours. (When the collars are removed the additional height will mimic the appearance of traditional baked soufflés.)

Cherry sauce Melt the butter and sauté the cherries for 3 minutes, Add the sugar and the kirsch, Carefully ignite the latter to burn off the alcohol and continue cooking for 8 minutes, allowing the sauce to thicken. Transfer to the refrigerator to cool.

Presentation Just before serving sprinkle the top of each soufflé with brown sugar and quickly caramelize it with a kitchen torch. Remove the foil collars and center the soufflé mold on a serving plate. Serve with the chilled cherry sauce.

Warm almond frangipane tart with white chocolate sauce

Serves 10

Pastry crust
300 g (10 1/2 oz) finely milled semolina flour
125 g (4 1/4 oz) almond flour
125 g (4 1/4 oz) granulated sugar
125 g (4 1/4 oz) unsalted butter
1 egg
1 egg yolk

Almond frangipane
125 g (4 1/4 oz) almond flour milled from
unpeeled almonds
125 g (4 1/4 oz) granulated sugar
125 g (4 1/4 oz) unsalted butter
3 eggs
1 dl (scant 1/2 cup) rum

Chocolate sauce
100 g (3 1/2 oz) white chocolate
100 g (3 1/2 oz) heavy cream
50 g (1 3/4 oz) calvados

Garnish
powdered sugar
almonds
cinnamon sticks

Equipment
10 tart pans 10 cm (4 inches) in diameter
with removable bottoms
1 circular cutter 12 cm (5 inches) in diameter

Pastry crust Combine the two types of flour and the sugar; add the butter (slightly softened), the whole egg and the egg yolk. Blend well to form a smooth dough; enclose in plastic wrap and allow to rest in the refrigerator for 1 hour. Roll out the dough to a 1/8 inch thickness and cut out ten 12 cm (5 inch) circles. Use these to line the base and sides of the tart pans. Prick the dough with the tines of a fork and bake in a preheated 180° C (356° F) oven for 15 minutes.

Almond frangipane Place the almond flour, granulated sugar and butter in a mixer and beat at low speed for 30 minutes, adding the eggs at 10-minute intervals. At the 28-minute mark incorporate the rum. When the beating process is complete, refrigerate the mass for 3 hours.

Chocolate sauce Break the chocolate into small pieces and heat it with the cream in the upper portion of a double boiler. When completely melted, incorporate the calvados, remove from heat and cool. Refrigerate until ready to use.

Assembly Fill the pastry shells with the almond frangipane and bake in a preheated 200° C (390° F) oven for 9 minutes; cool slightly and carefully remove from tart pans.

Presentation Nap each serving plate with the chocolate sauce, top with an almond tart, dust with powdered sugar and garnish each with almonds and a cinnamon stick.

Duo of strawberries with basil ice cream and vanilla infused extra virgin olive oil

Serves 10

500 g (1 lb) cultivated strawberries
500 g (1 lb) wild strawberries
50 g (1 3/4 oz) granulated sugar

Vanilla infused extra virgin olive oil
1/4 lt (1 cup) extra virgin olive oil
2 vanilla beans

Caramelized olives
100 g (3 1/2 oz) pitted taggiasche olives*
100 g (3 1/2 oz) granulated sugar
100 g (3 1/2 oz) water

Basil ice cream
8 egg yolks
250 g (8 3/4 oz) granulated sugar
80 g (2 3/4 oz) glucose (available in pastry supply stores)
1/2 lt (2 cups) milk
1/2 lt (2 cups) heavy cream
80 g (2 3/4 oz) fresh basil

Garnish
fresh basil

Infused oil Split the vanilla beans and immerse them in the oil. Conserve at room temperature for 48 hours.

Caramelized olives Place the olives in a small saucepan with the sugar and water. Simmer over low heat until the water has completely evaporated and the sugar has caramelized. Cool completely and then chop the olives.

Ice cream Beat the egg yolks with the sugar until light. Incorporate the cold milk and cream and bring just to a boil. Cool, add the glucose and the finely chopped basil. Transfer to an ice cream machine and freeze according to manufacturer's instructions.

Presentation Rinse both types of strawberries. Quarter the cultivated variety and mix them with the wild strawberries, the chopped olives, the sugar and a little of the infused oil. Crush a few of the berries to release their juices and insure that the ingredients blend well. Place two tablespoons of the mixture in the center of each plate, top with a quenelle of the ice cream and decorate with basil leaves and a few drops of the infused oil.

* Cultivated in the Liguria region, these tiny olives have a distinctive nutty flavor.

Basic recipes

INFUSED OILS AND EMULSIONS

Basil-infused extra virgin olive oil

2 dl (scant 1 cup) extra virgin olive oil
1 bunch fresh basil

Purée the basil with the oil in a food processor or blender. Strain through a fine-mesh sieve (discarding the solids) and reserve the oil.

Green marzullo tangerine-infused extra virgin olive oil

2 dl (scant 1 cup) extra virgin olive oil
zest of 1 green marzullo tangerine

Macerate the tangerine zest in the oil for 6 days, filter and reserve.

Mint-infused extra virgin olive oil

2 dl (scant 1 cup) extra virgin olive oil
1 bunch fresh mint

Purée the mint leaves with the oil in a food processor or blender. Strain through a fine-mesh sieve (discarding the solids) and reserve the oil.

Wild fennel-infused extra virgin olive oil

1 dl (scant 1/2 cup) extra virgin olive oil
50 g (1 3/4 oz) wild fennel

Purée the wild fennel with the oil in a food processor or blender. Strain through a fine-mesh sieve (discarding the solids) and reserve the oil.

Black oil

100 g (3 1/2 oz) pitted black olives dehydrated in a preheated 80° C (175° F) oven for 4 hours
100 g (3 1/2 oz) extra virgin olive oil

Purée the olives with the oil in a food processor or blender; filter and reserve.

Hot pepper and vanilla infused extra virgin olive oil

2 dl (scant 1 cup) extra virgin olive oil
1/2 vanilla bean
10 g (1/3 oz) sugar
pinch of salt
pinch of hot red pepper

Split the vanilla bean, scrape out the seeds and emulsify them with the oil, sugar, salt and hot red pepper. Allow to infuse for 5 hours before using.

Orange vinaigrette

10 g (2 tablespoons) extra virgin olive oil
1 tablespoon white wine vinegar
juice of 1 orange
salt, pepper

Emulsify the oil with the vinegar and orange juice; salt and pepper to taste.

BROTHS

Veal broth

1.5 kg (3 1/3 lbs) veal short ribs
4 lt (4 quarts) cold water
1 onion
2 carrots
2 celery ribs
a few cloves
1 clove of garlic
salt, black peppercorns

Place all of the ingredients in a large stockpot and cover with the water. Bring to a boil; reduce heat and gently simmer for 3 hours, skimming any impurities that rise to the surface. Do not salt the broth too liberally as successive reduction will concentrate the flavor. Filter the broth through a fine-mesh sieve; cool and refrigerate. Remove any fat which has collected on the surface of the chilled broth, repeat the filtration process and refrigerate again until ready to use.

Quail broth

Proceed as above, substituting the quail bones and trimmings for the veal.

Vegetable broth

1.5 lt (1 1/2 quarts) water
1 onion
1 leek (white portion only)
1 carrot
2 celery ribs
1 small bunch flat-leaf parsley
butter or extra virgin olive oil
a few cloves
1 bay leaf
salt, black peppercorns

Roughly chop the vegetables and parsley and sauté them in the butter or oil until softened. Cover with the cold water; add the cloves, bay leaf, salt and peppercorns. Bring to a boil, reduce heat and simmer for 1 hour skimming any impurities that rise to the surface. Filter the broth through a fine mesh sieve; cool and refrigerate. Remove any fat which has collected on the surface of the chilled broth and refrigerate until ready to use.

Fish fumet

2 lt (2 quarts) water
700 g (1 1/2 lbs) heads, bones and trimmings from non-fatty fish
1 onion
1 leek
1 celery rib
butter or extra virgin olive oil
1 small bunch mixed herbs (flat-leaf parsley, basil, thyme, bay leaf, marjoram)
black peppercorns

Roughly chop the vegetables and sauté them in the butter or oil until softened. Add the fish, herbs and peppercorns and cook for 5 minutes. Cover with the cold water, bring to a boil, reduce the heat and simmer for 20 minutes skimming any impurities that rise to the surface. Cool, filter and refrigerate until ready to use.

STOCKS

Veal stock

3 lt (3 quarts) water
1 kg (2 1/4 lbs) veal bones and trimmings
100 g (3 1/2 oz) carrots
100 g (3 1/2 oz) onions
50 g (1 3/4 oz) celery
1 clove of garlic
150 g (5 1/3 oz) fresh tomatoes
1 teaspoon tomato paste
1 small bunch mixed herbs (flat-leaf parsley, basil, thyme, bay leaf, marjoram)
salt

Crack the veal bones and roughly chop the trimmings. Brown them in a 250° C (480° F) oven (or in a Dutch oven over a high flame). Add the roughly chopped carrots, onions and celery as well as the garlic clove and continue browning for 30 minutes. Transfer to a stockpot and add the tomatoes, herbs, tomato paste and salt. Cover with the cold water and bring to a boil. Reduce the heat and simmer for 4-5 hours, skimming any impurities that rise to the surface. Take care that the bones are never exposed and add water to cover if necessary. Filter through a cheesecloth lined sieve and reserve.

Lamb stock

Proceed as above, substituting lamb bones and trimmings.

Duck stock

Proceed as above, substituting duck bones and trimmings.

GARNISHES

Fried tomato skins

Wash the tomatoes, remove their skins in quarters, blot them dry on paper towels and fry them in 130° C (266° F) extra virgin olive oil for 1 minute.

Fried basil leaves

Carefully wash the basil, blot the leaves dry on paper towels and fry them for 1 minute in 130° C (266° F) extra virgin olive oil. Drain on paper towels.

Fried leeks

Reduce a leek to a fine julienne approximately 8-10 cm (3-4 inches) long, blot dry on paper towels and fry in 130° C (266° F) extra virgin olive oil for 4-5 minutes or just until golden.

Candied ginger

Peel 30 g (1 oz) of ginger root and reduce to a fine julienne. In the meantime prepare a syrup by dissolving 10 g (1/3 oz) of granulated sugar in an equal amount of water. When the syrup begins to color, add the ginger and toss to coat.

SAUCES

Pesto

40 fresh basil leaves
1 dl (scant 1/2 cup) extra virgin olive oil
1 pinch kosher salt
2 cloves of garlic
20 g grated *pecorino* cheese
20 g grated *Parmigiano reggiano* cheese
40 g pine nuts (fresh or slightly toasted)

Place all of the ingredients with the exception of the oil in the work bowl of a food processor or blender and process until you have obtained a smooth, homogenous paste. With the motor running, add the oil in a thin stream and continue processing until all of the oil is completely blended.

Cuttlefish sauce

5 dl (scant 2 1/4 cups) dry white wine
1 onion, chopped
5 dl (scant 2 1/4 cups) heavy cream
1 packet squid ink
100 g (3 1/2 oz) butter
salt

Place the onions in the wine and reduce to 1/4 its original volume. Strain through a fine mesh sieve and transfer to a small saucepan. Add the cream and squid ink and simmer for a few minutes. Continue cooking for 1 minute while whisking in the butter and the salt.

Tomato sauce

1 kg (2 1/4 lbs) peeled, crushed tomatoes
2 tablespoons extra virgin olive oil
50 g (1 3/4 oz) onion, chopped
1 tablespoon butter
pinch of sugar
bay leaf, flat-leaf parsley, rosemary, sage, thyme
salt, pepper

Sauté the garlic and onion in the olive oil. Add the tomatoes, sugar and salt and pepper to taste. Simmer over medium heat for 45 minutes. In a separate pan, sauté the herbs in a little butter and olive oil. Filter off the fat and add the herbs to the tomatoes near the end of the cooking process.

Green sauce

10 g (1/3 oz) chopped flat-leaf parsley
1 hard boiled egg
10 g (1/3 oz) brine-cured capers, rinsed
2 anchovies preserved in oil
10 g (1/3 oz) extra virgin olive oil
salt, pepper

Finely chop the parsley, egg, capers and anchovies by hand. Emulsify with the extra virgin olive oil, salt and pepper to taste and refrigerate until ready to use.

OTHER PREPARATIONS

Cous cous

Serves 8
300 g (10 1/2 oz) cous cous
4 dl (scant 2 cups) water
fish fumet or veal broth (depending on the final use
of the cous cous)
extra virgin olive oil
butter
salt

Spread the cous cous on a rimmed platter and quickly work
in half of the water and a drizzle of extra virgin olive oil,
runnng the grains through your fingers to separate them.
Fill the base of a couscousier with the fish fumet (or veal
broth) and bind the rim with a clean kitchen towel. Transfer
the cous cous to the upper perforated compartment and
set it over the lower portion. Heat the couscousier over a
medium flame.
After approximately10 minutes, steam will begin to escape
from the chimney. At this point, use a wooden spoon to
spread the cous cous once again on a rimmed platter. Work
the grains with a circular motion, taking care that they do
not form lumps. As soon as the cous cous has cooled
enough to handle, gradually pour over the remaining cold
water and another drizzle of extra virgin olive oil. Run the
grains through your fingers to separate them and then
return them to the perforated compartment of the
couscousier.
Repeat this process twice more at 10 to 15 minute
intervals, then lightly salt the cous cous. The entire cooking
process should take approximately 45 minutes.
Transfer the cous cous to a serving platter and fluff the
grains yet again. Season with a little melted butter and a few
ladles of fish fumet (or veal broth). Cover with a damp cloth.
The grains will continue to plump. Keep warm until ready to
serve.

Fresh egg pasta

200 g (7 oz) semolina flour
200 g (7 oz) all-purpose flour
6 egg yolks
1 whole egg
10 g (1/3 oz) salt
1 tablespoon extra virgin olive oil

Mound the sifted flours on your work surface and create a
well in the center. In a bowl beat the eggs, egg yolks, salt
and extra virgin olive oil to combine them and pour into
the well. Begin drawing the flour over the egg mixture with
your fingers, gradually amalgamating the liquid and dry
ingredients. Continue kneading the mixture until all of the
ingredients are well combined (approximately 15 minutes).
The dough should eventually achieve a smooth, elastic
texture. Gather it into a ball, enclose it in a damp cloth and
allow to rest in the refrigerator for 1 hour.

Traditional orange granita

1 lt (1 quart) water
1 kg (scant 2 1/4 lbs) sugar
1 lt (1 quart) freshly squeezed orange juice

Place the sugar and water in a heavy bottomed saucepan
and heat over a medium flame until the sugar has
completely dissolved. Cool, blend in the orange juice,
transfer to a shallow container and freeze. When the
mixture begins to set, grate the ice crystals with a fork at
30 minute intervals until the desired consistency is
achieved.

Orange Tuiles

(for 20 tuiles)
100 g (3 1/2 oz) unsalted butter
200 g (7 oz granulated sugar)
juice of 1 orange
grated zest of 1 orange
65 g (2 1/3 oz) all-purpose flour
125 g (scant 4 1/2 oz) chopped almonds

Melt the butter over a double boiler, cool and reserve. Beat
the sugar with the orange juice, add the melted butter, the
grated orange zest, the flour and the chopped almonds,
whisking vigorously to blend all of the ingredients. The
batter should be creamy, but still liquid. Drop even
tablespoons of batter on a parchment lined cookie sheet
and bake in a preheated 170° C (338° F) oven for 8
minutes. Cool and store in an airtight container.

Index